Chains of Grace

PETER JEFFERY'S STORY

© Day One Publications 2008
First printed 2008

ISBN 978-1-84625-127-6

British Library Cataloguing ivn Publication Data available
Unless otherwise indicated, Scripture quotations in this publication are from the **New International Version** (NIV), copyright ©1973, 1978, 1984, International Bible Society. Used by permission of Hodder and Stoughton, a member of the Hodder Headline Group. All rights reserved.

Published by Day One Publications
Ryelands Road, Leominster, HR6 8NZ
☎ 01568 613 740 FAX 01568 611 473
email—sales@dayone.co.uk
web site—www.dayone.co.uk
North American e-mail—usasales@dayone.co.uk

Published jointly with Solid Ground Christian Books
PO Box 660132
Vestavia Hills, AL 35266, USA
http://solid-ground-books.com
Phone Toll Free (866)-789-7423

Cover design by Kathryn Chedgzoy
Printed by Gutenberg Press, Malta

Peter Jeffery, 1990

Jeffery family in Rugby, 1977

Peter and Lorna Jeffery, 1997

September 1937	Peter is born in Neath
From 1939 to 1945	World War 2 takes place
September 1954	Peter starts going to church with Lorna
May 1955	Saved by God's grace
March 1956	Starts National Service in the RAF
March 1958	Finishes National Service
March 1958	Peter marries Lorna
April 1959	Gaynor is born with spina bifita
September 1960	Enters college
June 1961	Diane is born
July 1963	Ordained and starts at Ebenezer, Pontnewydd, Cwmbran
January 1964	Pauline is born
April 1967	David is born
September 1972	Ministry commences at Rugby
February 1982	First trip to Australia
March 1984	First operation
August 1985	First heart attack
September 1986	Ministry commences at Sandfields
January 1992	Heart bypass operation
June 1992	First trip to USA
January 1995	Retires after second heart attack

Contents

UK Foreword by Neville Rees

I met Peter when he spoke in the open air for the first time, and as young people from Neath, Skewen and Port Talbot, we began friendships that would continue.

First and foremost, Peter is an evangelist who followed Paul's directive to Timothy to 'do the work of an Evangelist' (2 Timothy 4:5). Wherever he went, throughout this book, which is his life story, gospel preaching, testimonies and church growth feature. As A W Tozer identified true worship as the lost jewel of the Evangelical Church, so the diamond that makes the Evangelical Church shine and glitter must be gospel proclamation and witness.

What makes the New Testament Church? We read throughout the Book of Acts that 'the Word of God grew and multiplied' and that 'they went everywhere preaching Jesus and the resurrection'. Have we forgotten that the Bible's overall message is about the personal work of Jesus Christ? Yes, there are many spokes that reach the community life but basically the hub is that men and women are born, live a span and die. 'Why are we here?' and 'Where are we going?' are the two major questions they may and, indeed, must ask. The answers are one: Jesus Christ. We are to know him whom to know is eternal life.

I commend this easy-to-read journey of a man who found Jesus Christ and wants to tell others about him. Peter Jeffery has done that and still is doing it through this book and others. Thrown into the bargain are real questions on true preaching, what it is, and true conversions which are clearly and simply answered and explained.

Neville Rees, retired pastor, Morriston, Swansea, Wales

USA foreword by Steve Martin

I count it a great privilege to write a foreword to Peter Jeffrey's autobiography. It is like a mouse writing a commendation for his friend, the lion.

I have used most of Peter's books with great profit, especially to give away to students, for beginning Christians of all ages, for home-schooling parents looking for great material for children, for senior citizens just beginning to read for spiritual profit, to spiritual inquirers, and to others. I have given away hundreds of Peter's evangelistic booklets and hundreds have disappeared off of our literature rack in the foyer of the church. God has used Peter in my life and in my church's life.

I want to thank God for Peter's speaking and writing ministry for four reasons:

First, Peter aims at simplicity. One of the marks of our Lord's ministry according to Mark's Gospel was that 'the common people heard him gladly' (Mark 12:37, KJV). Spiritual discernment was required, but the Lord did not make a spiritual hearing of the truth more difficult by speaking in thought forms the people could not readily understand. Thank the Lord that this is one of Peter Jeffery's best gifts. Most people do not realize it until they have to communicate something, but the simpler you make something, the harder you must work as a communicator. Take any one of Peter's books and you can give it to any Christian and many non-Christians and they can understand it. Bravo Peter!

Second, Peter aims at clarity. A speaker or writer can be simple and yet not be clear. That is why it takes so much work (and it is a gift) to be both simple and clear. So whether you are reading *Opening up Ezekiel's visions* or *Christian Handbook* or *Seeking God*, you know exactly what he is saying. He works hard at illustrating the truth with large windows to let in the light, 'windows of truth' as he likes to call them. He doesn't flood his preaching or writing with illustrations, nor is his communicating an extended illustration in search of a text! His ability to give apt illustrations makes the truth clear and always drives home his points.

Third, Peter is biblically faithful. One has never had to worry that Peter might teach the right truth from the wrong text. He shows his mastery of the basics of biblical understanding in his helpful primer, *Stepping Stones*. He shows his mastery of the basics of church history, Christian theology and how we got our Bibles in *Christian Handbook*. He shows how to make basic Christian doctrine applicable to life in *Bite-sized Theology*. The best men in church history have turned their learning into holiness and usefulness for Christ and his Kingdom. The biblical notion, 'Thy Word have I hid in my heart', has become, for too many, 'Thy Word have I hid on my hard drive!' Books come easily today; godliness does not. Christian maturity is obedience to truth over time. Peter has walked with God and he has wrestled with God in prayer for the Holy Spirit's accompaniment when he preaches and writes.

Fourth, for Peter, the main thing is to keep the main thing as the main thing! Peter aims at conversion by keeping the gospel as the centre of his ministry. Peter is hungry to see people come to know the living Saviour who changed his life over fifty years ago! Peter aims at conversion. Peter wants young Christians to grow up to honour and enjoy Christ for ever. You cannot read such books as *I will never become a Christian* or *Seeking God* or *Salvation-Exposed* or *From Religion to Christ* and not feel his heart throb. As Europe and America are written off as post-Christian by too many 'top men', we must pray that our gracious God, who loves to save sinners, will raise up an army of young men with Peter's gifts again.

Steve Martin, Pastor, Heritage Church, Evangelical-Reformed-Baptist, Fayetteville, Georgia, USA

Foreword

Ordination, 1963

The Beginning

In the 1920s and 1930s, Neath was a small industrial town in the heart of South Wales. The Neath valley had many coal mines and it was not unusual at the end of a week to see black-faced miners coming into town to collect their wages from the office of the local coal owner. It was a town with a long history going back to Roman times and Neath castle and Abbey go back to 1130. There was not much of a spiritual history until Frank and Seth Joshua came to the town in 1882 to establish a gospel work. A remarkable work was done as God mightily used their preaching.

In the 1950s and 1960s, God raised up in the town about a dozen young evangelical preachers who, as well as preaching in their own land, would take the gospel to many parts of the world. I was privileged to be one of those men.

I became a Christian on Saturday May 21, 1955, at the age of seventeen. I spoke in public for the first time the following Friday when I gave my testimony at an open-air meeting in Neath. During that summer I gave my testimony of salvation several times at meetings in my home town of Neath. By the winter I had begun to preach and, looking back now, this was quite ridiculous. I did not know enough as an eighteen-year-old to preach, but people in the church recognized that I had the 'gift of the gab' and encouraged me to preach. I have to admit that I did not take much encouraging because from the beginning I loved to preach.

For the first fifteen years of my life, I had been sent to Sunday School, but I had never been taken to church so I was over seventeen before I ever heard a sermon preached. It was meeting up with a lovely young girl in the factory where I worked that first got me to attend a Sunday evening service. Lorna was to become my one and only girlfriend and, in the course of events, my wife. She encouraged me to attend her church, the Green Mission in Neath.

Chapter 1

It was there, in September 1954, that I first heard preaching from Pastor Ben Rosser. He was a lay pastor but an excellent Bible expositor and for eight months I listened to him every Sunday evening.

In May 1955, Billy Graham was preaching at Wembley Stadium in London and a special train was going up from South Wales on the Saturday. I agreed to go, not to hear Billy Graham, but to see the famous Wembley Stadium! As a seventeen-year-old, I was sports mad and this was my only reason for going. In fact I can vividly remember saying to Pastor Rosser's wife, as we went to catch the train, 'I will never become a Christian.' Thankfully, God knew better and, on May 21st 1955, I was saved.

From then on I began to attend the Green Mission regularly with Lorna. We went to the Prayer Meeting on Tuesdays, Christian Endeavour on Thursdays and services on Sundays. It was in the Christian Endeavour meeting that I first spoke to children and first preached. I dread to think what I must have preached in those days because, as I have said, I did not know enough to be a preacher. Other churches invited me to preach and I bought a long black overcoat and a black Bible bag so I looked the part, but I should not have been in the pulpit. I should have been listening and learning.

Many years later I came across a verse in Ezra that summed up the preacher for me—'For Ezra had devoted himself to the study and observance of the Law of the LORD, and to teaching its decrees and laws in Israel' (Ezra 7:10). Ezra first learnt the Word, then he lived it and only then did he begin to teach it. This was not done in a few weeks but must have taken years. A teenager preaching should be the rare exception, and certainly not the rule. Often Charles Spurgeon is mentioned in objection to this principle, but I was no Spurgeon, and few people are.

By March 1956, my preaching was forced to take a halt as, like all eighteen-year-olds in those days, I was drafted into the Forces for two years' National Service. I spent two years in the Royal Air Force. Like most young men, I did not want to go, but now I can see that those two years were a better preparation for the ministry than the three years I was later to spend in theological college. Living with twenty men in a barracks really threw me in at the deep end. In those early days I was the only Christian and it was a case of either 'sink' or 'swim'! Later on I met some fine believers and learnt greatly from them.

I was demobilized in March 1958 and married Lorna the same week. I started preaching again and was quite happy in the role of lay preacher. I was not happy in my job as a tool setter but had no thoughts of the ministry. Then our first baby was born in April 1959. She had spina bifida and only lived nine days. Apparently there was more spina bifida in South Wales than anywhere else in the world.

My first experience of the death of a person was at the age of fifteen, when my father died. I will never forget that Friday in October 1952. It was the most happy and the most sad day of my life up to that point. My father was keen on sport and always encouraged me to play. So when that day in school I was told I had been picked to play rugby for Neath schoolboys the next day against Cardiff, I was overjoyed. I was given the famous Neath black jersey and could not get home quick enough to show my father. He was ill in bed, and I had no idea how ill he was, but by the time I arrived home he was dead. Shock, anger and numbness were emotions that seemed to explode in my mind all at the same time. I was not a Christian and had no God to turn to. Death was so cruel, pointless and final.

When death came a second time into my life I was a believer but it still hurt. Both Lorna and I were devastated, but quite independently God spoke to both of us in this great time of sorrow calling me into the ministry. The call was unmistakable and in September 1960 I entered Memorial Congregational College in Swansea to train for the Christian ministry.

It was a typical denominational college, liberal in theology and taking the University of Wales course in theology. We learnt very little biblical theology, but there I developed a love for church history under the lectures of Dr Pennar-Davies. Of the thirty students, about six were evangelicals and together we learnt our theology from the emerging books published by the Banner of Truth and from the writings of Dr Lloyd-Jones.

Those were the days when you could buy Puritan books very cheaply in the second-hand book shops in Neath and Swansea. I remember buying ten volumes of Matthew Henry's New Testament in mint condition for a shilling (5p) each, Calvin's Institutes at 5 shillings (25p) for two volumes. It was these treasures that began to give substance to my preaching.

In the last term of college, the minds of all the students began to turn to which church may call them as pastor. This was particularly a problem for evangelicals. The evangelical students were very popular in the

Chapter 1

Congregational churches of South Wales. This was because they could at least preach with vigour and enthusiasm unlike most of the other students, but listening to their message every Sunday was another thing. The Moderator of the denomination told me that because I was an evangelical I would never get a church in Wales. I asked him about Ebenezer, Pontnewydd in Cwmbran where a well known evangelical, Derek Swann, had just finished after seven years as pastor. He told me that he had spoken to this church and that they had enough of evangelicals and would never call another one. This was not true. He had spoken to only one man in the church who had vigorously opposed Derek Swann's ministry all along. When this church began to show an interest in calling me, I told them what the moderator had said and they were amazed. Derek's ministry had been greatly appreciated by them. This was the church that called me and in the summer of 1963 I started as pastor at Cwmbran.

With Lorna in New Jersey

Family

A pastor needs a good wife to stand alongside him in the work. It is a rare man who can manage on his own. I was fortunate because God gave me the best. Lorna could not preach a sermon or lead a Bible study to save her life, but if there was a family in the church in trouble, she was the first one there with practical help. In this she was a tower of strength and the church folk loved her for it.

Pastor and wife are a team and we were no exception. This was seen in our call into the ministry. Through the death of our first daughter, Gaynor—she had spina bifida—God spoke very clearly to both of us independently. We both knew what the will of God was. There was no need for discussion; it was clear that the Lord wanted us in the ministry. And by and large it has been like that for over fifty years. I could not have survived in the pastorate for five minutes without Lorna!

The forty-three books I have written were all written longhand and then Lorna typed them and got them ready for the publishers. In the early days this was done on a portable typewriter and it was a lot of work. A computer makes it easier but I still cannot type so I depend on Lorna for this. Without this teamwork, the books would never have been written.

In the first years in the work, we always seemed to be short of money. Every young pastor was. We tried desperately not to let this affect the three children too much, and some families in the church were very kind to us, but every summer, when holiday time came around, we felt this keenly. We discovered that it was impossible to have a holiday at home. Sooner or later I would be working. So we decided to scrape all the money together that we could, and buy a tent. At least then we could get away every year on holiday! It was a good idea but it did not last long. Every time we put the tent up or took it down, it rained. This was demoralizing for a family who were not really campers. It came to a head one night when we were camping at Woolacombe; a gale blew and I was up all night hanging on to the tent pole and it was just as well I did because the tent next to us blew away. So that was the end of our camping adventure.

Diane, Pauline and David were three very different children but they all contributed to a lively household as they grew up. They wanted a dog, so we got them Taffy, a delightful mongrel. Soon after we had him, there were screams from the lounge. Taffy had rounded up the three children on the settee and would not let them down. After that, it was a long time before they would walk on the floor again—they preferred to crawl from chair to chair!

Children grow up and soon the girls were bringing boyfriends home. Eventually this led to marriage—Diane first, and then Pauline. Several months after Pauline's wedding reception, we received a letter from the hotel saying that they could find no record of our having paid the bill. We knew we had paid but they would not take our word for this, so we needed the receipt. We had put it safe—so safe that we could not find it. There was no way we could pay again, so the search for the receipt was intensified. At last we found it and all discussions about whether or not the bill had been paid was settled. The receipt was the irrefutable answer.

I used that incident several times in sermons.

As sinners, we had a great debt. We had broken the law of God time and time again, but the great message of the gospel is that Jesus has paid that debt for us and the proof, the receipt, is the cross. Paul tells the Colossians that God 'forgave us all our sins, having cancelled the written code, with its regulations, that was against us and that stood opposed to us; he took it away, nailing it to the cross' (Colossians 2:13,14). It is as if there is a great bill with our name on it which lists all our sins; but Jesus has taken that bill, paid it for us and nailed it to the cross, which is the equivalent of stamping it 'paid in full'.

As Christians, we still sin and Satan comes to us to us and tries to rob us of assurance. John Newton, the former slave dealer who by the grace of God became a preacher of the gospel, must have known much of such accusations. With all his past as well as his present sins, Satan would tempt him to ask how he could be a Christian. Don't we all know something of this? But Newton knew how to answer Satan:

I may my fierce accuser face, And tell him thou hast died.

He had the receipt of his salvation, namely the cross. When you are attacked like this, wave the receipt in the face of Satan. He has no answer to the blood of Jesus.

BIRTHDAYS

Birthdays are always happy times in families, and two stand out for us. My mother's birthday was February 28th. This particular year she was eighty-two years old and my daughter Pauline phoned up to wish her Nanna a happy birthday. She told her that she had a special present for her—a new great-grandson. My mother did not believe her because Pauline was not due to have the baby for a few weeks. She took some persuading that Pauline was phoning from the hospital and the baby had been born on her birthday.

In September 2007, I turned seventy years old. I had no idea what the family had planned as a celebration, but apparently everyone in our church knew except me. Diane and Phil, her husband, came to take me out to tea but they would not say where we were going. I thought we were going to my son's house, but we passed the turning for there and before long we were going over the Severn Bridge and into England. I thought it was rather a long way to go for a cup of tea! Three hours later we arrived at a magnificent country house in Dorset where all my children and grandchildren had gathered for a long weekend to celebrate my birthday. The house was magnificent, the weather was glorious and I had the best birthday ever.

**Eldest grandchildren—
Jonathan and Christopher**

**Grandchildren—Jamie,
Sam, Abby and Becky**

Bala camp team of officers in the 1960s

Cwmbran, 1963–1972

By the time we went to Cwmbran, our daughter Diane had been born, so the three of us started a new phase in our lives. I was then twenty-five years old.

Ebenezer Congregational Church, Pontnewydd, was in the new town of Cwmbran. They were a warm and welcoming people and we soon settled happily among them. For the first time in my life I had to prepare two sermons and a Bible study every week. This meant that I spent six mornings every week in the study. The afternoons were given to pastoral visitation and the evenings were given to meetings. This was to become the pattern I was to follow for the rest of my ministry. I started work on sermons on Monday mornings which meant that I lived with a sermon for a week before it was preached.

Sermon preparation took a great deal of time. One reason for this was that I had become a slave to a system of every sermon having to have three points and a conclusion. And, of course, each point had to have a suitable title in alliteration. I found I was spending as much time working out the alliteration as I did on the exposition. After a few years, I dropped three points and alliteration and developed a sermon pattern that suited me better. I have nothing against the three points way, but I found that it was not, except on rare occasions, for me.

Young preachers need to give a great deal of thought as to how they want to preach. I have always been a text preacher. I would start with a text, expound it, apply it and finish with it. Exposition and application are essential in any sermon, whereas structure and outline can vary from preacher to preacher. My advice to young preachers would always be this: develop your own style and do not be afraid to break away from the party line. But never forget that the purpose of your preaching is to confront men, women and children with God.

Lay preaching with a different congregation every Sunday is nothing like preaching to the same people week after week. Your preparation has to be much more careful and illustrations cannot be repeated. But such preaching is much more satisfying. To be able to say to a congregation at the end of a sermon that you will take up this subject again the following week is a real blessing. And to preach a series of sermons on a Bible book stretches both you and your hearers.

CAMPS

In the mid 1960s, I was invited to be the preacher at one of the Evangelical Movement of Wales' Camps at Bala. This was the first of many weeks at camp in years to follow. It was my responsibility to preach at the daily service. Most of the seventy or so young people were not Christians so it was an excellent opportunity for the presentation of the gospel.

As the week went on, it became clear that something was happening that we thought was of spiritual significance. By the end of the week, about twenty young people had made a profession of faith and I and the other leaders were thrilled and excited. We had not put undue pressure on the people attending the camp, but the very atmosphere of camp had put its own pressure on the young minds.

The following year most of the same youngsters were back in camp and it was clear that they were not actually saved. Emotion is no substitute for conviction and repentance and, from that experience, I learnt a great deal about dealing with souls. It was becoming clear to me that you do not pick little green apples. Let me explain the analogy:

During the first twenty years of our married life we lived in four different houses. They were nice enough places, but not one had much of a garden. So it was a real joy to move into our fifth house, which not only had a nice garden, but also three mature apple trees.

The first autumn saw a magnificent crop of apples and we were determined to save as many as possible. So after they were picked, we wrapped each one separately in newspaper and stacked them all on wooden trays in the garage. We looked forward with anticipation to apples all the winter. By Christmas they were all rotten.

I spoke to a farmer friend about this and he said it was because I had picked them too soon. I protested that they looked ripe. Yes, he said, but did they come easily? He explained that the right time to pick apples is when they come away from the branch easily into your hand. 'If you have to tug, leave them,' he said. 'They are not ready for picking and will go rotten.'

That was good advice on picking apples, but it is also good advice on dealing with the souls of men and women. How often in our churches have we been overjoyed to see people make a profession of faith, but, within a short time, it becomes obvious that they are not saved and soon they stop attending church. This is so dishonouring to God. It is a cause of deep disappointment and frustration for us as Christians, and it very often makes those who made the profession very hardened against the gospel. They say, 'I was saved—and it does not work.'

It is a very real problem. The modern 'invitation system' aggravates it, but even in churches where this system is not used, and where more care is taken in dealing with souls, it still happens. Why is this so? Often, like my apples, it is ignorance coupled with enthusiasm. We are so eager to see souls saved that we ignore basic biblical principles. As a consequence of this, we hurry souls to a decision before they are ready. How can we know when the right time has arrived to pick spiritual fruit?

Firstly, we must always remember that a true conversion is not the result of human decision but a work of the Holy Spirit. There are evidences of this divine work. We read in Acts 11:23 that at Antioch, Barnabas saw the evidence of the grace of God. The prime evidence is always conviction of sin, which will lead to repentance. There can be no salvation without this. Conviction will vary in degree from one person to another, but it must be there.

In past generations Christians used to make a distinction between a soul awakened and a soul saved. By 'awakened' they meant that the Holy Spirit was beginning to deal with the person. Conviction was coming and a longing for pardon was being created. But this was not yet conversion. Perhaps we today ought again to make this distinction and not try to hasten the work which the Holy Spirit is beginning.

This does not mean that we should sit back and do nothing. If you see signs that God is awakening people, then pray for them. Help and advise, but let the Holy Spirit do his own particular work. Like the ripening apples, they will come easily and no pressure will be needed. There are no rotten apples in a harvest that is reaped by the Holy Spirit of God.

I have never asked people to come forward and repeat the sinner's prayer. I have never used decision cards and rarely have I 'led a soul to the Lord'. But many souls have been saved. I just preach and leave the Holy Spirit to do the rest. Often it has been weeks after someone was saved that I came to know about it. I am happy with this because I believe that the Holy Spirit is the best counsellor.

BLESSINGS AND CRITICISMS

A preacher is always looking to see converts. I had learnt from the pattern set by Dr Martyn Lloyd-Jones to preach to the believers in the morning and to unbelievers in the evening service. By the time I had retired, this pattern had reversed and we would see more unbelievers in the morning service, but still one service every Sunday was evangelistic. So the desire to see fruit from the gospel preaching was always there. At Ebenezer, the first convert came about three months after I started when a sixteen-year-old girl was saved. The following May, a young man was saved and later on it was my delight to conduct the marriage ceremony of these two, and later still to preach at the man's ordination to the ministry.

The converts came slowly but steadily and the church began to grow. But the preaching also upset some people and one deacon resigned after I had been there for about six months because he said I was making Paul into a pope. He did not like the New Testament epistles and also said that he could not believe that someone would go to hell simply because they were not saved. Ebenezer was an old established congregational church and several of the deacons and many of the members were not born again. I am sure that many did not understand the gospel even after seven years of outstanding preaching from Derek Swann and then from my own efforts. They were lovely folk but thought that church attendance was all that God required.

One deacon complained that all I ever preached was the need for people to be saved. I had to point out to him that he only ever came to church on a Sunday evening when I preached this way, and he was neither there in the morning service nor the mid-week Bible study when the ministry was for believers. The problem with many of the older folk was that they could not see the need of the gospel for themselves. When the sixteen-year-old girl was converted, she went excitedly to tell her grandmother, a member of the church. Her granny was very annoyed because she thought that her granddaughter did not need to be saved. In her view, she was a good girl and salvation was only for wicked and immoral people.

Years of religion inoculated people against the gospel and this is very difficult to counteract. The Bible has no authority in the lives of these folk. They may well like you as a person and admire the hard work you put into the church, but they cannot understand the gospel. Preaching to people like this is not easy. I can remember a lady in Ebenezer who used to listen to me with a smile of incredulity on her face. Obviously she was amazed that I still believed the teaching of the Bible. As far as I

Peter with children's meeting, 1965

know, only one of the older people in church was saved under my ministry, but there was an encouraging work among those under forty years of age.

I myself was only twenty-five when I was ordained, so perhaps it is not surprising that I was more able to reach the younger folk. However, the main barrier was not age so much as years of listening to religious teaching that never mentioned sin or the new birth. In the 1960s, most young evangelical pastors in their first church in the denominations were the first Bible men the church had had in the pulpit in living memory. I was fortunate in that I followed Derek Swann who had, for seven years, preached the truths I wanted to preach. In spite of this, the church was very much a congregational one and not an evangelical one. It took another nine or ten years from my successor, Philip Williams, before the church could be honestly be described as evangelical.

LEARNING

During these years I was learning how to preach. I believe that preaching is a gift that God gives and if God has not given it, then the man in the pulpit will never be a preacher. But if the gift is there, it has to be developed and this may take years. Preparing two sermons every week and preaching them to the same people is part of this learning. It can be hard sometimes on the congregation as mistakes are made, but the folk at Ebenezer were very tolerant with me. Not only does a person's style and delivery of the sermon improve, but also his doctrine develops and I found that I was more of a Calvinist at the completion of my ministry in Ebenezer than I was when I commenced there.

As you get established in a church and become known as a preacher, invitations come to you to preach elsewhere. In 1966, when I was still only twenty-eight, I preached for the first time at the Aberystwyth Conference of the Evangelical Movement of Wales. Over the next thirty years, I was to preach many times there, but that first time was the most nerve-racking. I was due to preach on the Thursday evening and, for the whole week, I was a bag of nerves. I could not enjoy the conference at all as my mind was taken up with the coming Thursday. Preaching at Aberystwyth was always a daunting experience but nothing compares to that first time.

I remember one year preaching at Aberystwyth and waking up in the middle of the night in tears praying for the hundreds of young people who would be listening to me the next evening. I think it was that year that I preached on 'Whitewash' from Ezekiel 13 and in the mercies of God several listeners were saved.

CONVERTS

There were converts at Ebenezer but not a great number. One day some of the men in the church were discussing why there were not many converts. One young man said, 'Perhaps the Lord cannot trust us with them.' That was a very sobering thought. Are we too prone to make converts clones of ourselves and fill them with our prejudices and criticisms? Are we reluctant to let the Holy Spirit do his unique renewing work in these spiritual babes? If so, then we had better sort this out quickly before the church dies around us.

A middle-aged man began to attend church regularly. He had no Christian background whatsoever, but appeared to be very interested. A lady in the church was convinced he had been recently converted and urged me to speak to him. I did so and as we spoke of the reason why we needed to be saved, he readily acknowledged that he was a sinner but then added, 'But I am as good as the next man.' When he said these words my heart sank. A sinner in whom the Holy Spirit is at work will never talk like that. He had no concept of personal sin and guilt and was definitely at that moment not converted. In fact, I don't know if he was ever saved.

Sometime afterwards, this man's son began to attend. He was in his early twenties and had returned home after living in London. He told me something of the life he had lived in London and was convinced he was too sinful to be saved, but within a few weeks he was converted.

Here was an interesting contrast: a father who had no conviction of sin and his son who was the exact opposite. There can be no salvation without conviction and repentance and so it was not surprising that one was not saved and the other was.

A woman came every Sunday with her three sons, the eldest of whom was seventeen. The boys obviously came because they had to, and they showed no interest in the gospel, but after a while, it became apparent that the elder boy had been saved. The story he told me was quite interesting. He said, 'You know I only came to church because I had to and every Sunday I was bored, especially during the sermon. One Sunday I was so bored that I decided to listen and God spoke to me and I was saved.'

People are bored in church very often not because the preaching is bad but because they do not listen. When they listen, boredom disappears and then anything can happen.

COFFEE BAR

In the 1960s we started a coffee bar at Ebenezer. This was not particularly well equipped or decorated, and just had tables and chairs, free coffee and biscuits and about twenty very keen Christians to run it. We printed invitations and circulated them in the schools and coffee bars of the town. We were amazed how many youngsters came. Here is an article I wrote in 1966 for the Evangelical Magazine of Wales on Coffee Bar Evangelism.

Chapter 3

Coffee Bar Evangelism

This type of evangelism had never been tried in our area until last September when a team of students came to conduct a ten-day campaign. It was they who started the work and every night of the campaign any number up to a hundred teenagers crowded into the Coffee Bar. When the students left we felt constrained to carry on this work, and so, every week since, on Monday night at 9 p.m., the Coffee Bar has been open. There is no doubt in our minds that this work has been owned of the Lord, and that He has led us to bring the Gospel to young people in this way.

When you think of a Coffee Bar, perhaps you imagine some ultramodern place with a juke-box, etc, but our Coffee Bar is far from that. It is just the schoolroom of a chapel (40 feet by 20 feet), about half a mile from the town centre where the teenagers gather. The furniture is just that which is normally used for Sunday School work. I mention this to show that it not necessary to have ideal premises for this work; the premises are not half as important as the workers.

We are a team of about twenty Christians, mostly young, who really feel called to this work. It was pointed out to us when we started that there is no substitute in God's work for consecration and faithfulness.

The value of complete dedication is obvious, but very often we, Christians, forget the value of faithfulness. This is vital in Coffee Bar work. It is no good being there one week and away the next. This is soon spotted by the teenagers and unfaithfulness in Christians can be a real stumbling block to unbelievers finding faith. I think that one of the main impressions that our 'customers' have come to see is that we are concerned about their souls, and that this is the only reason we are there every week to speak to them about the Saviour.

When we started the work we went out to the town 'fishing' and brought the youngsters to the Coffee Bar. Now we find they come along without having to be brought and there is an average attendance of about fifty; a substantial proportion of these are the long-haired, leather-jacketed boys, who seem to have no interest in the usual teenage pastimes of youth clubs, sport, etc. Quite a lot of them have been in trouble with the police and a few have got themselves entangled with 'purple-hearts'. These boys are rapidly becoming the outcasts of society; they rarely hold a job for any length of time and just drift through life aimlessly.

Recently a few of them left the Coffee Bar one Monday night and stole a car for 'kicks'. Afterwards a policeman remarked, 'You are wasting your time with that lot,' but if we believe that Christ died for 'that lot' we just cannot leave them to their sin. Whether they know it or not they need Christ desperately and it is Christ whom we seek to present to them.

The presentation is very simple—no gimmicks, no gadgets—just sitting around in groups with a cup of coffee and a biscuit talking about Jesus. Two things soon become obvious in talking to them—firstly their willingness to listen, and secondly, their almost complete ignorance of the Scriptures.

This willingness is very encouraging, especially when we see them coming back week after week to talk; we know that some only come because the coffee is free, but most come to talk about God. Some just love to argue, but even then, behind all the arguments, it is sometimes possible to see a longing for what they see we have found in Christ.

We have been engaged in Coffee Bar Evangelism for nearly six months and so far we have seen very little results in the way of conversions. There has been one profession of faith, and a few come to Sunday services now and again. It's a long-term work, requiring patience and faithfulness and often we leave the Coffee Bar feeling exhausted and disappointed, but our confidence is in the Lord. We believe that He is going to glorify His Name in the hearts of these teenagers. Some are deeply convicted, and have said so openly that they are afraid of being converted because of what their friends will say. Some even refuse to come to the Coffee Bar because they are afraid of being converted. These boys and girls abound in any village or town in Wales, and very often they are not being reached with the Gospel. They won't come into our meetings, but that doesn't mean they are past redemption. We have got to go out to them with the Gospel of Christ. A Coffee Bar is one way of reaching them. It isn't the only way, but it is the way along which the Lord has led us.

For we know, brothers loved by God, that he has chosen you, because our gospel came to you not simply with words, but also with power, with the Holy Spirit and with deep conviction.

1 Thessalonians 1:4, 5

Salvation at Cwmbran

LINDA

I longed to be part of the church, to really belong there. So I tried desperately to be 'spiritual' and for a few years I worked really hard at being a Christian. In July 1963 Peter Jeffery came to the church as our new minister, and I heard the gospel preached every Sunday evening. After the service the young people would go to the manse and often spent time talking about the sermon we had just heard. I was still trying to be a Christian, but the harder I tried, the more I failed.

In early October the Lord graciously opened my ears to really listen and hear the gospel. At last I could see that no matter how hard I tried, I could not make myself a Christian.

When we got to the manse that evening, I spoke to Pastor Jeffery about needing to ask God to save me. We spoke for a while and then I prayed, confessing my wasted efforts and bringing my sin to God for forgiveness. Immediately I knew that God had forgiven me and that I was his child. I was now a Christian. I was sixteen years old then and now, at the age of sixty, I can honestly say that the Lord has kept me and blessed me. Life has not always been easy. There have been many problems and illnesses, but in everything the Lord has been with me.

I believe that the Lord gave me a husband who was tailored for my particular needs. He has been a pastor for twenty years and we have had the privilege of serving the Lord together.

Chapter 4

NORMAN

I had just left the chapel after morning service, and I was in real distress. The invitation had been given for anyone who trusted and served Jesus Christ as Saviour and Lord to remain and share in that Communion.

But that didn't apply to me and I knew it. I desperately wanted to be saved, but what could I do? Deep down I felt that there was more to faith than me just deciding to believe. God must do something, but I didn't know what or how. So I left before the Communion. I sat in my car and desperately called to God. 'If you will not save me, I can't be saved. If you will not help me, I can't believe. I've got nowhere else to go. Please!' In that moment I knew I had been saved. All the barriers seemed to disappear, and a load I had been carrying for months was gone. It was Whit Sunday 1964.

My gospel journey had started a long time before that. I had been brought up in the chapel and had attended services and Sunday school most of my life. In the mid-1950s, Rev Derek Swann came as pastor and, even in my early teens, I knew that this man's preaching was different. He actually explained what the Bible said. He talked about Jesus being God, about sin and about Jesus coming to save us from sin. Through my teens I realized that what he was saying made sense. People were being saved. I had come to believe that what was being preached was true. The only way to be saved from sin was through the death of Jesus Christ. But so what?

By the time I had reached the end of my teens, I was only attending church occasionally and then I stopped going altogether.

But the gospel haunted me. My conscience wouldn't give me any rest and I couldn't find purpose or satisfaction in anything. I have often described my life then as one big 'If only'.

In the meantime, Peter Jeffery had been called to the pastorate, and I was attending from time to time. Although in personality and style he was different from Derek Swann, he preached the same message with the same earnestness. The gospel was beginning to get through. By then it was early 1964, and an incident occurred which left me more hopeless than I had ever felt, and I can still remember saying, 'From now on, Lord, I want you.'

From that time I went to every church service and the prayer meeting.

I read my Bible avidly at home. I attended any and every meeting where I knew I would hear the gospel.

I didn't need to know the gospel; I needed to believe it for myself. I needed God to take hold of me. And that brings us back to where we came in.

Now some forty years later, I'm sitting in my study writing this testimony and thinking that it's about time I went out to visit some members of my congregation. Twenty-three years after being saved, the Lord called me out of secular work and into pastoral ministry.

Oh that the Lord will show the same mercy and grace through my ministry that he showed to me through Derek Swann and Peter Jeffery.

BOB

It was August 18th 1970 when I first trusted in Christ. I was then twenty-one years old. At the time, I was working as a labourer with a team of brick-layers in Newport. I began to experience a terrible emptiness within myself. The futility of life began to get to me, because I soon realized that no matter how hard I worked, or how much money I earned, I was never going to be satisfied.

One Saturday night I went to a dance hall in Cardiff, and I came out the worse for wear in a drunken state. I walked past a water fountain near Cardiff Castle (it's still there today) and it had a  Bible text inscribed on it: 'Whoever drinks of this water will thirst again, but whoever drinks of the water that I shall give him, will never thirst.' (John 4:13–14).

I read those words and felt so challenged by them, that when I returned home I took out the Bible and began to search for them. I began to read the Bible on a regular basis; I read about this man Jesus in the Gospels and repeatedly came to the cross. I could not understand that if this man was who he said he was, why he was crucified. It became a stumbling block in my mind. After this I began to have desires to go to church to learn more, but which one?

As we drove home from a day out, I stopped at the traffic lights at Mon Motors. I looked up and saw the Ebenezer Church and a small voice seemed to say, 'Go in there.' Later I returned to the church, but as I approached the doors I hesitated, thinking I was taking all this a bit too seriously, so turned around and went to the pub. Because the Holy Spirit had spoken to me I felt convicted; I had no peace. So I began to bargain with God saying that if he would spare me until the following week I would attend the church.

I did live for another week and so went to the church. Peter Jeffery was the preacher then, and he preached the gospel as if he really believed what he was saying. That spoke to me and I soon realized that I was a lost sinner. Every night after this for five weeks I prayed this prayer: 'Lord forgive my sins and show me the path of righteousness.'

Even though I prayed that prayer I felt no assurance, and could not say that I was saved. In fact, I felt too bad to be saved and that Jesus could not save me.

On the way home from a meeting, a young Christian couple invited me for coffee. I shared with them that I had been praying, but still could not say that I was saved. The husband asked me a question: 'What was the first thing that Jesus said to do, when he came preaching? The message was this: repent and believe.' I felt this was the last nail in the coffin. I looked up to him and said in my heart, 'But Lord I have believed and repented.' I returned home that night feeling worse than ever. As I knelt for prayer that night, suddenly the Lord's light flooded my soul and I was saved.

People say that religion is for weak people, and that it is a crutch. But I have found it to be the biggest challenge of all. To follow Christ and to put into practice his teachings every day is challenging. But is the most blessed life and I would not have it any other way.

**The opening of the new baptistry
at Rugby**

When it all nearly finished

I had been at Ebenezer for eight years with no real problems. Often in ministers' meetings I had heard other pastors tell of the serious difficulties they were facing in their churches. I knew nothing of this, until in 1971 a gigantic problem exploded in my ministry.

My church was a congregational one, which meant, among other things, that it practised infant baptism. For a few years I had been having doubts about this but kept these doubts to myself. Then in 1971 I knew that I really held believers' baptism views and was convinced that I had to share this fact with my deacons. They saw no problem as long as the church continued to baptize infants and they felt things should continue as before. But two men in the church did not agree. They were not deacons but were trustees and they quoted the church trust deed that the pastor had to be a paedo-baptist. This deed also referred to the 1833 Congregational Declaration of Faith which was what the church was to believe and practise.

Although I had been pastor there for eight years, I had never seen this declaration. In fact, neither had anyone else in the church! When eventually I read it I was pleasantly surprised because it was Calvinistic in its doctrine and I believed it all except for three words. These words were in the section on baptism and said that 'baptism should be administered to converts to Christianity *and their children*'. This was enough to have these two men start legal proceedings to close the church because I was in violation of the trust deed.

One of these men was the deacon who had resigned and he was not really interested in the Declaration of Faith. He just hated the gospel and had once told me that, as he put it, the rot started in Ebenezer when Derek Swann came as pastor. He saw an opportunity to get rid of me and the gospel, and he seized it with both hands. I told him that if I was to be removed for not believing three words of the 1833 Declaration, then whoever followed me would have to believe it all and therefore would have to be a convinced Calvinist.

The other man was different. He was a born again man but seemed to have a bitter distrust of Baptists. He was convinced I had a secret plot to turn Ebenezer into a Baptist church.

The last six months of 1971 were extremely difficult. For the first time in my life I was in a situation I could do nothing about. In desperation one evening, I phoned Dr Martyn Lloyd-Jones for advice. I had been in many conferences where the Doctor (as he was affectionately called) was the speaker, but I had never spoken to him personally. When he answered the 'phone I explained who I was and that I had a serious problem in the church. To my amazement he said he knew who I was and he knew all about my problem. He went on to say that in a few weeks' time he would be preaching at the Heath Church in Cardiff and he would see me between the afternoon and evening services.

I went to Heath wondering if he would remember, but as soon as the afternoon service was over, one of the church elders came to me to tell me that the Doctor was waiting to see me. He gave me an hour of advice that was both helpful and encouraging.

The church at Ebenezer did not want me to go and came up with all sorts of ideas to get around the problem. One was that I should be employed not as pastor but as caretaker and still preach on Sundays. By January 1972, however, it was clear that the two men would close the church on legal grounds. I could not allow this and so I resigned as pastor.

I was to work six months' notice and these were the most difficult six months of my life. I came to hate Sundays and did not want to preach. No other church seemed interested in calling me and I resolved to leave the ministry and become a probation officer. The whole business of ministry and preaching had gone sour and this situation continued for a couple of months until God, in his mercy, began to lift the cloud. I began to see again that I was called to be a preacher and not a probation officer, but still no church was interested in my being their pastor.

It happened like this. Over the Easter period, the Evangelical Movement of Wales was holding a rally in Swansea. A friend of mine, Andrew Davies, was preaching and Lorna and I went along. Andrew said nothing that dealt directly with my problem, but he preached with great power and authority. I felt the Lord was saying to me, 'This is what you should be doing, not probation work.' Immediately there was kindled in my heart again the desire to preach. I believed that the Lord had not yet finished with me as a preacher.

When we got home from Swansea, there was a letter waiting for me from Aston University informing me that I had been accepted to train as a probation officer. So the door was not yet closed on this. I really wished it had!

I was convinced the Lord wanted me to preach, but circumstances seemed to contradict this. I was married with three children and I had to support my family. I could not afford to be out of work. For the next five or six weeks still no church showed any interest in my being their pastor. This went on until June when two churches suddenly began to show an interest.

One was a Baptist church in Crewe and the other was the Evangelical Free Church in Rugby.

My preference was Crewe and the deacons there were unanimous in recommending to the church that they call me. But the vote in the church meeting did not bring the required majority. This left Rugby which was a much smaller church and had recent serious problems. By then I knew the probation service was not for me and when Rugby called me I had no hesitation in accepting. God had closed one door and so we walked through the one still open. We—my wife Lorna and by now our three children, Diane, Pauline and David—did not know then that the next fourteen years were to be ones of rich blessing. They were years not without their problems but these were far outweighed by the mercies of God. By the end of August we were living in Rugby and my preaching began to know a new power.

Looking back at this time of doubt and confusion I have come to see that as far as I am concerned circumstances alone are not a good indication of God's will. I needed something else. I needed the Holy Spirit bearing witness with my spirit as to what God was saying. Sometimes circumstances confuse this and they can test faith almost to breaking point. Circumstances were telling me to be a probation officer. God was saying be a preacher and by now my heart was wanting what God was saying. But God kept me in confusion until the week before I was due to start at Aston when Rugby called me to be their pastor.

Peter Jeffery, Rugby, 1986

Rugby, 1972–1986

In September 1972, I began my ministry in England. This was surprising for a biased, one-eyed Welshman who when it came to the game of rugby supported two teams—Wales and whoever was playing England! We had heard so much about cold, reserved Englishmen but that was soon shown to be a myth. The folk at Rugby received us with warmth and enthusiasm. They loved to hear the Word preached and gave rapt attention to the sermon. I believe that a congregation can either make or break a preacher and Rugby Evangelical Free Church made me a better preacher than I had been before.

Suddenly a new power and authority came into my preaching and this was more than the enthusiasm of my listeners. A few years later, we had a visit from a missionary and after the service she was talking to a new batch of converts—young men in their twenties. She came to me and asked if I had been baptized in the Holy Spirit. I thought this was a strange question, but she went on to say that after talking with the young men it was obvious that something remarkable was going on. I said no, I had not been baptized in the Holy Spirit. I said this because I was thinking in terms of tongues and healings etc, but I now believe I was wrong. I had been baptized in the Holy Spirit. I knew nothing of tongues, but the power that had come upon my preaching could only be explained in terms of the work of the Holy Spirit.

We started in September 1972 with a congregation of about fifty. By Christmas it was a hundred and by the following Christmas it had grown to two hundred. In a few years, over three hundred were in attendance and eventually we planted three new churches fifteen to twenty miles around Rugby, at Long Buckby, Leomington and Banbury. The growth was so staggering that some other churches in the town did not like it. They accused us of sheep-stealing. One of our elders had a marvellous answer to this—'We don't steal sheep; we grow grass.'

I loved to grow grass, that is, to preach to the spiritual needs of believers. Our initial growth was not so much from converts but Christians who came to us from local Methodist, Anglican and Brethren churches. These were people who, for years, had been starved of spiritual food. One man who had been for ten years in the Pentecostal church told me that in all that time he had never heard the word 'justification' mentioned from the pulpit. Preaching that does not deal with the great biblical doctrines will never feed the souls of believers. It may entertain or even excite, but will not feed. Growing grass ought to be a top priority for all preachers. There is a marvellous example of this in Nehemiah 8:8, where it is recorded that 'They read from the Book of the Law of God, making it clear and giving the meaning so that the people could understand what was being read.'

There is more to preaching than this—application, exhortation, challenge etc—but if at the end of the sermon the people have not understood the passage under consideration, then the preaching process has not been happening properly. The expounded word should speak to the needs of the people. One Sunday morning, a lady phoned me to tell me that she had three serious problems she needed urgently to talk to me about. I suggested that she should come to me after the morning sermon to arrange a meeting time. After the service she did come to see me, but said there was no need for a meeting because her three problems had been answered in the morning's sermon. To this day I don't know what her problems were, but God knew and dealt with them through the preaching of his Word.

Feeding the flock was done primarily in the morning service when systematic preaching through various books of the Bible was undertaken. As well as this, series of sermons on subjects like Revival, the Attributes of God, and the life of Peter both instructed and challenged the listeners. The evening service was always evangelistic and our folk were not slow to bring their relatives and friends to hear the gospel.

1979

From the time I began at Rugby in 1972, we had seen remarkable things from God, but in 1979, conversions had all but come to an end. This greatly disturbed me because I believed that the gospel was designed by God to save and so it ought to save. I did not know what was wrong. Was it that we had become too proud of the blessings and forgotten the Lord? Had the Lord turned his back on us? In this frame of mind I went in June to the Evangelical Movement of Wales Conference for ministers at Bala. In the prayer meetings at Bala, God really dealt with me and I learnt afterwards that he dealt with certain other men like Bob Cotton of Bury St Edmunds. I felt God was saying that we had become too complacent and were taking him and his work for granted. Immediately on my return to Rugby, I called a special meeting and put all this to the church. I called the church to prayer for forgiveness and to intercede that the Lord would give us conversions again. I believed the church had become lifeless and that few were being converted because there were few unconverted people at the services. I urged the church to consider Isaiah 62:6–7 'You who call on the LORD, give yourselves no rest, and give him no rest ...' In response to this challenge, a letter was sent out to every member by the elders and deacons, and the prayer meetings were stirred to a spirit of prayer for the lost.

In the following October, we had church anniversary meetings arranged when the preachers were to be Dr Lloyd-Jones, Vernon Higham, Andrew Davies and others. We decided to make these meetings evangelistic and to pray earnestly that the Lord would use them. God began to answer our prayers immediately, and, long before the special meetings came, we began to see conversions again. Within a very short time, people started arriving at the church through all kind of circumstances and from every sort of background,

In the church at Rugby

and over the next fifteen months, God graciously gave to the church the encouragement of many conversions.

A period of remarkable blessings began which stretched well into 1980. Some folk in the church felt it was a mini revival. I would not put it as strongly as that though it certainly was a special work of grace.

As well as conversions through the normal preaching, the Lord was working in some young men in their twenties whose whole existence was bound up in the drug and pop scene. Two of these were converted as we were praying for conversions but they were unknown to us and they began attending church that summer as men already saved and anxious to learn of God. In February 1980, we baptized thirteen of these converts. The same month, one of our young men was killed on a motor cycle on his way to college. Apparently five were saved at his funeral service.

These were remarkable days.

CHAINS OF GRACE

It was here that we saw chains of grace beginning to interlink. Someone would bring a relative or friend who would be converted and, in turn, bring more relatives and friends. Whole families were saved in this way.

A deacon was very concerned for his brother, an unbeliever, and asked the church to pray for him. One Sunday he came to church and, before long, he was saved. His teenage son was amazed at what had happened to his previously atheistic father. He came, and he was saved. Then the mother and sister were saved. This was one of our wonderful chains of grace. Here is the testimony of the father.

> My wife and I attended the church in Rugby at the invitation of my brother. It was at the end of 1979 when we went for the first time and heard Pastor Jeffery preach from the Book of Romans. After the service, I told my wife that we would not be going to this church again because I was very offended at what I heard. The following Sunday, we went to another church to see if they were the same as the Rugby one, but we were not offended in any way.
>
> Then the Sunday after, we found ourselves back in Rugby because over the two weeks I found that I was starting to remember the sermon I had not liked in the first service, and

also the hymns I had not sung were constantly coming back to my mind. I was aware from the start that my life was changing. I stopped doing many things I had become ashamed of. From then on, we became regulars at the church and our son came with us.

Early in 1980, I was being convicted of my sins and, shortly after that, I was converted. I came to love the Word of God and I still do. Later on, our son was converted and we were both baptized in the same service, along with twelve other people. A year after we first came to the church in Rugby, my wife was converted, and in the next year, both my daughters were saved. All five of our family are now in the family of God.

A young man brought his brother who was in the sixth form of the local grammar school. He was saved, then he brought his friend who was converted the first time he came to church. Soon the friend brought his sister and she was saved.

Perhaps the most unusual chain of grace involved Chinese students. In the 1970s and 1980s, many Chinese students came from Hong Kong to Rugby to do their 'O' and 'A' level examinations in preparation for university. Through various means, many of these came to church, and, between 1978 and 1983, a total of fifteen Hong Kong Chinese students were saved and baptized. These Chinese believers had a great concern to reach every Chinese man and woman in the area with the gospel. On one occasion, they asked me if they could use the schoolroom for an evangelistic meeting on a Saturday afternoon for the Chinese folk. I readily agreed and offered that the church should finance this effort. They politely refused the offer as they wanted to do it themselves. A preacher was invited from the Chinese church in London and, on the given Saturday afternoon, the schoolroom was packed with Chinese from all over the Midlands.

One of the most interesting chains of grace started with a young man in his twenties who was saved before he came to our church. He was from the pop and drug scene and wanted to buy a tape deck to record his music. He saw one advertised in the local newspaper. He bought it and with it came some cassettes. Rather than record over whatever was on the cassettes, he decided to listen to them first. They were sermons of the Irish preacher, Willy Mullen. This young man had never been to church and never met a

Christian, so what he heard made a huge impact on his life. He was deeply convicted of sin and was saved. He thought now that he ought to attend church, but which church should he go to? At that time, the Lord caused him to meet a believer at work from the Rugby church and that is how he came to us. Soon he was bringing his friends and several of them made a profession of faith.

I remember, on one occasion, speaking to a group of these young men explaining the basis of a Christian life to them. When we got on to talking about baptism, their eyes nearly popped out of their heads. It was all so new to them and they were excited and thrilled by the whole matter.

One of the young men had been thrown out of his home by his parents because of his behaviour. He never worked, he drank a lot, and played around with drugs. He was a typical long-haired, denim-clothed young man of that time. He was saved and his parents were so amazed at the change in him that they decided to come to church to see what had caused it. They were both saved and eventually both father and son became deacons in the church.

These chains of grace were not the product of organized evangelism, but of believers doing what every believer ought to do, that is, to pray for friends, witness to them and bring them to church. At Rugby we were very evangelistic. We did door-to-door visitation, preached in the open air and organized special weekends of gospel preaching, but we saw relatively few conversions from these. I believe we should do these things, but the most effective evangelism is spontaneous—in this sense not directly organized— and takes place when Christians bring their friends to church. I knew that on any given Sunday evening there would be unbelievers present and this encouraged me to preach the gospel.

UNHAPPY

It was not all plain sailing and some folk were not happy with what we were doing. One family left because they did not like my emphasis on disciplined Christian living. They felt that the Ten Commandments were not applicable to believers. They were good folk and it was sad to see them go.

Another man told me that he was taking his family to another church because, though he had been attending Rugby Evangelical Free Church for six years, he considered he had only been blessed in one service. I felt that it was necessary to point out to him that those six years were ones of unusual blessing in the church and that over a hundred people had been saved. Was it not strange that he was not being blessed while souls were being saved?

The Billy Graham crusade 'Mission England' in 1984 also caused us to lose some members. They could not understand why we were not involved in it. I will deal with this in greater detail later.

CO-OPERATION IN EVANGELISM

When I went to Rugby in 1972, the churches were in the middle of preparing for a town-wide campaign called 'Good News for Rugby'. Every church in the town, including the Roman Catholic one, was involved—except the church I had come to serve. I was delighted to support the stance my elders had taken. Even though I had no problems with the preacher of the campaign, ecumenical evangelism seemed to me to deny the uniqueness of the biblical gospel. This was highlighted when the churches took the whole of the front page of the local free paper in order to advertise 'Good News for Rugby'. All the supporting churches were listed. The following week the Christadelphians took the front page and, under the title 'Better News for Rugby', went on to say that most of the churches listed the previous week did not believe the Bible. This charge was unanswerable because it was true and confirmed that the Rugby church had been right not to be involved.

For many years, the churches in Rugby seemed to have existed on campaigns. When I started there I was introduced to many people often with the comment that this person had been converted in the 'so and so campaign'. I found myself replying on one occasion in exasperation with the question, 'Doesn't anyone get converted in the churches?'

Our absence from 'Good News for Rugby' caused us to receive a lot of criticism, but this was nothing compared to what happened in 1984 and the Billy Graham 'Mission England' campaign. Between 1972 and 1984, we had gone on with our own evangelism which included regular open-air preaching, door-to-door visitation and special evangelistic weekends, but this did not prevent us being from labelled as 'the church which did not believe in evangelism'. For many Christians, evangelism means only one thing—a special campaign every ten years or so. Our position was that evangelism was one of the prime responsibilities of the church and should go on all the time. We did not object to a special effort from time to time, but we did object to cooperating in evangelism with churches which did not believe the New Testament gospel. We particularly objected to those who had made a profession of faith being sent back to non-biblical churches. 'Mission England' was to bring all this to a head.

I had been converted at a Billy Graham Meeting in 1955, so I would have loved to have been able to support 'Mission England'. Unfortunately like all Graham Crusades of recent years, this one was ecumenical.

In October 1981 I attended a meeting at Coventry to discuss the proposed visit of Dr Graham. Dr Walter Smyth of the Billy Graham Evangelistic Association was there to answer our questions. I asked him why enquirers were sent to non-evangelical and Roman Catholic churches. The fact was not denied and the answer turned out to be very unsatisfactory. Another evangelical minister asked why Billy Graham did not come to England seeking only the support of evangelicals. He went on to say that if Dr Graham had done this, we would all be with him. Walter Smyth replied that if we did that, we would lose half our support.

On May 6th 1982, at the request of my elders, I spoke to the Rugby church on why we would not be involved in 'Mission England'. The church produced three hundred duplicated copies of this talk as well as recorded cassettes. The idea was to confine these to church use only, but copies got out and circulated, particularly in the west of England. Apparently as a result of this some churches pulled out of 'Mission England'. This resulted in the 'Mission England' organizers in the West sending out a letter warning readers about those 'who stir up discord between brethren about keeping doctrine pure'.

I wrote to the writer of this letter saying, among other things, 'I find it very disturbing that whenever an evangelical questions something like "Mission England", he is invariably accused of lack of love and of not being interested in evangelism. You insinuate both in your letters. I can assure you that it is because I have a love for my Saviour, a concern for the glory of God, and a great desire to see the gospel affect our nation that the lecture was first given. I honestly believe that the confusion which is always the result of co-operating in evangelism with Catholics and Modernists is no help at all to the spread of the gospel.'

I was not concerned too much about what people in other parts of the country felt, but I was very concerned about how people in my church would react. The overwhelming majority stood with the leaders, but some could not see the issues we raised. When every other church in town was running buses every night to 'Mission England', the issues got lost in the excitement. It was sad but some left the church over this.

OLDER FOLK

Retired people in the United Kingdom have lived through very barren times with respect to the gospel. Most of them have never heard the good news about Jesus even if they have at one time attended church. At Rugby Evangelical Free Church, we were concerned to reach such people. In December 1973, we arranged a Senior Citizens' Carol Service followed by a Christmas Tea. A hundred and twenty folk attended as a result of invitations being taken to Senior Citizens' clubs in the town. We had arranged with the Gideons to have large-print New Testaments to offer these folk and fifty-five responded to the offer. Following this, a regular monthly Saturday afternoon meeting for the older folk was commenced in March 1974 and on average about seventy-five attended each month. This led to us taking

Sandfields Old Folks' holiday

a coach load on holiday each summer. It was commented after the first holiday that 'some thought they were Christians before the holiday, but afterwards were not so sure.'

The gospel was new to these older folk and some were saved by the grace of God. One was a woman who had been a church-goer but it meant little to her. She was fascinated by believer's baptism and wanted to be baptized. I told her that I could not baptize her because she was not a Christian. She was upset by this but there was nothing else I could do. One of the elders went to see her the following week and reported to me that in his opinion she was saved. So back I went again and discovered following my last visit she had indeed been saved and, at the age of eighty, she was baptized as a believer. She testified, 'In June 1976 in my own home I remembered a moment when everything suddenly seemed to go quiet and I was conscious of my sin then of the peace of conversion.'

YOUNG PEOPLE

As the congregation grew so did the number of young people who attended. We could have as many as seventy at the manse on Sunday evenings after the service. Those manse meetings were a delight as the teenagers contributed and asked questions. Not all of them were converted and, at one point, we were beginning to have some trouble with these. They would all sit on the gallery and during the sermon some became a nuisance with their whispering and giggling. One Sunday, I stopped in the middle of the sermon and started talking about the whispering gallery in St Paul's Cathedral in London. I explained how it was a tourist attraction and very popular, but I said we were not going to have a whispering gallery in this church. Then I went straight on with the sermon. We had no more trouble.

CO-WORKERS

I was blessed at Rugby with some of the finest men it was possible to work with. I really enjoyed elders' and deacons' meetings and came away from them excited and with renewed vision. We were men all going in the same direction. I believed that I must have had the best elders in England. I am sure that other pastors have felt the same way but it really is a great joy to be working with, not fighting against, the church leaders. These were spiritual and able men. I was a better preacher than any of them but there were other aspects of ministry at which they were much better at than I was.

By 1982, the church had grown so much that I desperately needed someone fulltime to help in the ministry. I could cope with the preaching, but the pastoral work was becoming more and more demanding. It takes the same length of time to prepare a sermon to preach to thirty as it does to preach to three hundred, but serving as pastor to three hundred is vastly more demanding. We needed a man who was not primarily a preacher and therefore not aching to be in the pulpit, but a man to visit the people and relieve me of some of the pastoral work.

The Lord supplied the exact requirement. Gordon Shaw worked as an engineer in Rolls Royce and was one of our deacons. He had no great desire to preach but had an amazing gift in working with people. He loved them and they loved him. One man said of Gordon with warm appreciation that 'he could carry on a conversation with a cardboard box'! I always felt that Gordon had the gift of the Spirit which Paul calls in 1 Corinthians 12:28, 'able to help others'. He worked alongside me for fourteen years as a pastoral worker during which time we worked in harmony and trust.

The work in Rugby was so special that I believe the Lord put together a team of men in leadership of great quality and integrity. Outstanding among these was David Morgan. It was his vision that brought the church into being and he was always an immense help to me. His death in 1983 was a great loss to the church.

UNUSUAL EVENTS

During one of the General Elections in the 1970s , quite independently, the agents of both the Labour candidate and the Conservative phoned me to say that their man would like to come to one of our morning services and they both offered to do the reading in the service. I said that we would be glad to see them but we would take care of the reading ourselves. They both came, not at the same time, and after the service I was talking to one of these politicians. He told me how busy he was on various committees etc, and this prevented him going to church as often as he should. But, he said, when he had the time he liked to go to the old parish church of the town. He enjoyed the tranquillity of the music and the stained-glass windows and felt relaxed. I said to him that that was not Christianity but that it was escapism. He replied that he had gathered that from the sermon he had just heard. It's amazing how many people think of Christianity as no more than an emotional aspirin.

On another occasion, a Christian lady, who did not attend our church, phoned me to say that she worked as a dinner lady at the local girls' grammar school and had been witnessing to one of the sixth-formers. This girl now wanted to come to church and so this lady wanted her to come to my church. She asked if I could arrange for some of our young people to meet the girl outside the church and take her in. I said that I would gladly do that but I asked why she was not taking her to the church she attended. Her reply was that if she did, her young friend would never hear the gospel because it was not preached at her church. I replied if that was the case, what was she doing at that church? A few weeks later, both the lady and her family came to us and became keen members.

Chapter 6

For a believer to be part of a church that never preaches the gospel is indefensible.

On one of my trips to preach in Spain, I took two of the young men from Rugby with me. One of them fell in love with a Spanish girl in the church, and she obviously felt the same way about him. So here were these young people very much in love but they did not speak the same language. They did their courting via translation by a missionary in the church. But as soon as we got back to Rugby my young friend immediately enrolled in evening classes to learn Spanish. Eventually they got married and became missionaries in Spain.

EXPLANATION

The years at Rugby were ones of amazing blessing and I have often tried to find some explanation as to why the Lord was so good to us. Why did he not call me to Rugby in the normal way instead of through all the anguish and pain of my last year in Cwmbran? I had many good friends in the ministry who preached as well as I did but they never seemed to know such church growth. I could not understand these things. I knew it was the Lord's doing, but why?

There is no doubt that a power came on my preaching at Rugby that I had never known before or rarely since. It is difficult to explain, but there were some Sundays when I seemed to be sitting in the congregation listening to myself preach. There were periods when I could not preach without at some point in the sermon melting into tears. One man prayed that the Lord would enable the pastor to preach through his tears. The people sensed these things and there was a great air of expectancy in the church. I knew of one family who would not go on holidays on a Saturday but waited until Monday. They were afraid that they might miss something remarkable that could happen on the Sunday.

One Sunday as I sat in the pulpit waiting for the service to begin, I felt an overwhelming sense of the presence of the Lord. I became fearful and withdrew and I believe at that moment I quenched the Spirit. Who knows what may have happened if I had yielded to the Holy Spirit and not withdrawn? What fools we are sometimes!

On another occasion we had gone a few months without a conversion and this greatly disturbed me. We called the whole church to pray for conversions again and on Whitsun Sunday I was led to say to the elders before we left the vestry for the service that I knew there would be conversions that night. I had never talked like that before, but I knew, and three souls were saved.

The only explanation for all this is God. I don't know why he did it but it was certainly his doing.

Rugby church at Bryntirion

Then the church throughout Judea, Galilee and Samaria enjoyed a time of peace. It was strengthened; and encouraged by the Holy Spirit, it grew in numbers, living in the fear of the Lord.

Acts 9:31

7 Salvation at Rugby

GARY

In the summer of 1982, I bought a mid terrace house in Rugby next door to two young ladies, and invited them to a house-warming party which they gently declined. Some weeks later, I noticed a church minibus next door but the penny still did not drop. After a while, these ladies asked me if I would like go to church with them. I declined the invitation but they continued to invite me and I did eventually agree to go. That first Sunday morning service was an eye opener—the minister did not have a frock or a collar, he read and preached from the Bible as if he meant it, there were no social issues or politics, the people were friendly, and the singing was amazing. I enjoyed this first service so much that I went to the evening service as well. The ladies had given me a Gideon Bible which I started to read. After I had  been attending church on a reasonably regular basis, I even dared to go to the mid-week prayer meeting where I heard for the first time someone pray for me and for my salvation.

Hearing someone pray for you is quite humbling, and over the next few months I started to experience things I knew nothing about. I remember when the minister was preaching, I felt as if he was speaking only to me. I felt as if I was a foreigner—and of course I was, as I was alienated from Christ because of my sin. The gospel was preached in this church every Sunday and I soon realized that I needed to have my sins forgiven and that Jesus was my only hope, and that he'd died on the cross to save people just like me who didn't deserve his love. Before I started going to this church, everything had always revolved around me. Everything I had achieved and gained in life I thought was down to my own hard work, but I came to realize it all meant nothing without Christ in my life. It was usual for me to use bad language, drink and do other things which are better not to be remembered.

I did ask the Lord into my life on a number of occasions but had not experienced any sort of change. Then, one Saturday morning, I 'happened' to bump into a church elder. He asked me how things were. What he really meant was 'Have you been saved?' or 'Have you asked the Lord into your life?' I said I had, so he reminded me of the Scripture (Acts 2:21) which states that everyone who calls on the name of the Lord will be saved. Immediately, a weight lifted from my shoulders and I felt as if I was walking on a cushion of air. It was amazing. Now, twenty-five years later, I am still constantly amazed at my Lord's patience, love and provision for me and my family, through both the good and difficult times.

JANICE

I had no idea how the Lord would answer me when, in despair, I prayed, 'Please help me God!' many years ago.

My childhood was spent very happily on various farms where my father was working. It wasn't easy for my parents, on agricultural wages, to feed and clothe my sister and me. It was a case of 'make do and mend' and of producing as much food as possible from our garden.

As youngsters we were sent to Sunday School, but our attendance became less frequent as the years went by. By the time I left school, I didn't give church a second thought. Things seemed to pick up when I was able to earn my own living and to buy some of the things for which I have always yearned. But it wasn't to last for long. Within three years, my mother was badly crippled by a stroke and I had to give up my job to care for her. As time went on, we found it more and more difficult to make ends meet, and as we came to Christmas I was feeling particularly depressed and it was then that my cry went out to God. I thought that the answer, if there  was to be one, would come in the form of a win on the football pools or something similar. In fact, it came in the form of a dream that I should be married in the coming year, and so it turned out. This in turn led me to attending church. As my husband was a Christian and attended regularly, he always insisted that I should go with him.

When the Church opened at Railway Terrace, we were invited along and continued to attend whenever we could. I didn't listen a lot to what was being said, but the word 'sinner' was always cropping up. 'We are all sinners' was something I just couldn't accept. I couldn't see myself as a sinner, but I began to get more concerned about what would happen if I should die. I had heard many times that if I wasn't a Christian, I would go to hell. I was getting very worried and had many sleepless nights because of a growing awareness of my sin.

On June 13th 1976, I went to evening service as usual. Towards the end of the sermon, Mr Jeffery, who was preaching, said, 'It's so easy to become a Christian, even a child of seven can be one. Ask the Lord Jesus Christ now to save you.'

I felt as if he was talking to me alone, as if he knew my heart and as if no one else was there. My prayer went out, 'Please Lord, save me.' My heart seemed to miss several beats. The peace which came over me was tremendous and I knew without any doubt that my prayers had been answered. My fear of death, which had overshadowed me for so long, was gone. I felt so happy.

My life has taken on a new richness and I now enjoy fellowship with the Lord and his people. I have not found the Christian life restrictive. On the contrary, it is very full and free. My whole outlook is different now. I no longer want to do many of the things I did in the past, but these have been replaced by a desire to please the Lord. Death no longer holds any terrors for me, for God has promised that nothing will separate me from him, and when my time on this earth has ended I will live with him in heaven.

VALERIE

As I look back over the early years of my life (to the age of thirty-eight) I can only consider myself to have been a nominal Christian. I went to church twice on Sundays and sang in the choir until I went to university at the age of seventeen. From then on, my attendance was often irregular, even though I was studying the Bible and had been confirmed in the Anglican church. I twice taught in Sunday School at a later stage, but sadly the Bible was no more than a history book and I had no personal relationship with

Jesus Christ. Mercifully the Lord, who knows best for his children, had other plans for me.

Nine years after my marriage in 1956, I was diagnosed with severe rheumatoid arthritis. At the time my husband was involved with site work in Australia, so, with our two small children, we went to live there.

At first we rented a house in Sydney and, at this point, I came across a real Christian. She was a near neighbour and, on one occasion, she invited me to her home Bible study. The lady who was speaking took me by surprise by telling me that God was shouting at me through my illness. I wasn't offended—just rather puzzled—and acknowledged that because I'd always been accustomed to the set prayers of the Anglican church, I had not got the same freedom to pray aloud as the other ladies in the group.

Soon after that, we returned to England and settled in a village near Rugby. I knew I needed a change of church but didn't know where to begin. So I went back to the village one and for two years was longing for more Bible teaching. It was here that the Lord brought another real Christian across my path. She told me about the opening of an evangelical church in Rugby and tried to persuade me to go there. At first I was very unsure. However, in the end I relented and went to a ladies' meeting. At this meeting there was a missionary from Chile speaking about the life of Joseph. I knew I could identify with Joseph in all his difficulties and, when I heard the words 'and the Lord was with Joseph', I knew at last that I'd reached my spiritual home.

Now because of my pastor's good ministry, I began to have more spiritual understanding. The Bible was becoming more meaningful and I was surrounded by a great deal of Christian love and support. I was put into the care of an extremely helpful elder. As I was often housebound, he visited me on a weekly basis giving me quite a lot of spiritual guidance as well as encouraging me to read Christian books. In addition, he always came armed with a small suitcase to pick up some ironing. As a family we were very grateful as we were struggling very often.

There was still a major problem, however, that took me some time to come to terms with. I have a fairly active mind and my physical disability was causing quite a lot of frustration. In Australia, I had had a certain amount of physical freedom because of the mild climate but I lost this on my return to England so I found myself like the Israelites looking back and not fully appreciating that the Lord had a purpose in wanting me back in the UK. In 1980, I was finally brought to my senses by attending a Christian conference in Aberystwyth. The whole week was devoted to a study of the book of Jonah and it made me understand that I was just like the prophet if I was hankering after Australia. In other words, I had been wanting to go out of the Lord's will just for the sake of being physically active. As I am writing this I am aware how patient the Lord has been and how glad I am that the gift of repentance is ongoing. How thankful I am that the Lord is so good and faithful. I can truly say that his grace is (has been, and will be) sufficient for me.

MICHAEL

My parents sent me to Sunday school from an early age, though they never attended any church. When I was about fourteen, my father became very interested in Motor X and began to compete; all church attendance ceased. My parents, however, had moral standards and they brought me up according to the light they had.

I became very anti-Christian over the years and developed an unhealthy interest in the occult, taking part in many séances and using Tarot cards. On moving to a town close to the Welsh border, I somehow managed to 'lose' the cards. I never used them or took part in a séance again, though I still had a number of books on the occult. The place I moved to meant I was involved in regular heavy drinking and drug sessions.

I moved back to Rugby and met an old friend (John Lee). Though normally a depressive character, he seemed full of joy. I had no idea what had happened to him, but I wanted the same experience. One day John persuaded me to listen to the testimony of Willie Mullan. In what he had to say, Willie clearly demonstrated that there was a Saviour for sinners. I'd never heard anything like this before and it left me speechless. Although my life had not been quite like his, I could identify with it. Another time John made me listen to a message that urged commitment to Christ. John gave me a couple of books to read as by this time I was really seeking, though worried about all my occult books. (After I was saved, and had read about how the Ephesians burnt their occult books, I did the same.) One day I knelt alone before the righteous holy God. In September 1979, not knowing what to say—mindful there was no turning back—I opened up one of the books to the 'sinners prayer', making it my own prayer to God for salvation. At the Cross my burden was lifted—in just the same way as it was for Christian in the book *The Pilgrim's Progress*. Praise God, I was saved. This was all I knew— the Bible was true and Jesus was the Saviour. This happened without any contact with a church.

We bought Bibles and began to attend Rugby Evangelical Free Church. For the first time I encountered real preaching. The first time I entered, Andrew Davies was preaching and the awareness came powerfully to my soul that this was truth. Over the years, we were privileged to sit under the ministry of Peter Jeffery—ministry that powerfully lifted up the Lord Jesus Christ. This Christ-centred and cross-centred ministry formed a very important foundation for our faith.

All those years ago, a friend told me it would only last six months. The Lord Jesus Christ has not promised a trouble-free life, but he has promised to keep his people by his grace. My testimony, then, is that from beginning to end, 'Salvation is of the Lord.'

ADRIAN

'Amazing Grace! How sweet the sound, that saved a wretch like me!' These words of John Newton, the eighteenth-century slave trader who became a great evangelical preacher and hymn writer, are ones that I find easy to apply to my own life. Although brought up by good and loving parents in a moral and religious manner, I found during my late teenage years that there was something wrong at the very core of my being. I was religious, but I wasn't a Christian! However, in his mercy God not only showed me my problem, which was my sin against him, but he also showed me that he had already provided the solution, through the life, death and resurrection of  his Son Jesus Christ. I heard this good news during an anniversary service at Rugby Evangelical Church in October 1977. The preacher was Paul Bassett, the minister of Melbourne Hall in Leicester. It was a remarkable experience, as I felt that what was being said was solely for me and that the speaker seemed to know me inside out. I didn't 'decide for Christ' but was rather compelled to submit to him! I then joined the church at Railway Terrace where Peter Jeffery was the minister. These were formative years and the teaching I received and the evangelical books I was introduced to, such as the works of Dr Martyn Lloyd Jones, have stood me in good stead throughout my life.

I would like to be able to say that my Christian walk has been one of steady upward progress. However, after leaving Rugby I subsequently found myself living and working in the Reading area. It was during that time that I had a relationship with a non-Christian. This led to me falling away from the church and ultimately from Christ himself. While I was in this wilderness, I received a letter from my old pastor, 'PJ'. It was a loving rebuke, which certainly brought me up short. However, beyond the faithful wounds of a friend, is the amazing grace of God. In the summer of 1984, I decided to cycle the length of the United Kingdom from Land's End to John O'Groats. While I was on that journey, in the middle of the Yorkshire Dales having to have a buckled wheel repaired, I found myself sitting on a bus chatting with a young lady who was attending a nearby Bible convention. It turned out that she was struggling with doubts and as she told me about her problems, she turned to me and said, 'Are you a Christian?' Even as she spoke these words, I knew that I was, and that all that I had been doing could not extinguish the flame of life that God had lighted in me seven years previously. I came away from that bus trip facing in a new direction. I returned to church and, more importantly, to the Lord. Since then, in spite of my failures (and even my successes) God has continued to keep me. I now live and work in London, have a wonderful family, attend a local church and have many great Christian friends. But above all, I have a glorious future hope. And all of these blessings I owe to the amazing grace of God!

Sandfields church

8 Sandfields, 1986–1994

For years I had said that I would never go back to engage in ministry in Wales. I had seen more clearly the problems in Welsh evangelicalism on coming out from it and we were very happy in Rugby. But throughout 1985, there was a growing awareness that perhaps the Lord wanted me back in South Wales. I think a Welshman is more aware of his Welshness while living in England than he is while living in Wales. I wanted to go back and perhaps, in a small way, contribute to the work of the gospel in my homeland.

At this time I became aware that the church at Sandfields was looking for a new pastor. I preached there for the first time at a service especially arranged for New Year's Day, 1986. The church wanted me to go again, but I refused because I felt that one more sermon would prove nothing. My preaching was known well enough in Wales for the people to decide. I said I would meet with the church and answer questions. I did so and one of those questions was very interesting. I was asked whether I would return to Wales for a lower salary than I was being paid in England. I replied that my wife and I had talked about this and believed that we would have to take a considerable drop in salary if we returned to Wales. But, I added, why should this be so? Why were Welsh churches meaner to their pastors than English ones? There was a stunned silence, but the point was made and when Sandfields called me, they offered the same salary I was being paid in Rugby.

I started in Sandfields in September 1986 and the church responded warmly to my preaching. There was a teenage girl saved on my first Sunday there. Many in the church had been waiting for the sort of leadership and preaching I brought. Some did not like it and, early on, an elder resigned, but generally I was warmly received. When I left the church in January

1994, there were 144 members and 70 of those had come into membership during my pastorate. Not many of these were new converts but they were Christians who joined us attracted by the fact that we were still growing grass.

Sandfields had left the Presbyterian Church of Wales several years before I went there but I was amazed to discover how very much Presbyterian they still were at heart. I did not find this very easy to adjust to and perhaps I should have been more patient, but patience was never a strong virtue of mine. The church was dying—there were only about eight or nine children in Sunday School and there was no youth work at all, but they did not want to change anything. In spite of this we were encouraged. The church certainly grew and there were some converts. When I went to Sandfields I believed that I had a particular job to do. The slide the church had been going through for some years needed to be stopped and changes had to be made. Most people agreed with this in principle but when it came to detailed changes, it was a different story.

This was particularly true on the question of introducing a modern version of the Bible alongside the Authorized Version, and also the introduction of modern hymns. These, and other changes, were eventually accepted on the overwhelming vote of the church meeting, but they were never supported enthusiastically by many people. I have always believed in the value of the church meeting. When any serious change was proposed, it was first discussed thoroughly by the elders, then raised at a church meeting but never voted on until the following church meeting. This gave the members three months to pray over such matters before voting.

There was a lot of work to do and this took some time. We re-started the young people's fellowship, started lunches for the older folk, and a mothers' and tots' group was begun. For the first time, we had a Christmas

Playing bowls at Sandfields

Day preaching service and a carol service. An older folks' holiday was very warmly received and was held every year I was at Sandfields.

WOMEN'S WORKER

Jean Morgan was a member at Sandfields and for twenty-five years had been a missionary in Nepal. In 1993, she retired from missionary work and came back home to live in Port Talbot. In Sandfields we had between forty and fifty widows and we believed Jean should be called to work among these and the other women in the church. There was a real need there, and she had the gifts to meet it. The church was delighted to set Jean apart for this work and she proved to be a great asset to the pastoral work.

AMERICAN VISITORS

In 1992, I was preaching in Visalia in California and the pastor asked me if they could send a team to work with me for a couple of weeks in Sandfields. The following year six men and four women came for two weeks in April. They were like a breath of fresh air and the church took to them immediately.

They visited our folk in their homes, did schools' work and they themselves arranged to go into Swansea prison to speak to the prisoners.

One day we took them for a day out to Daniel Rowland's church in Llangeitho. We stopped for lunch at Lampeter and when our bus was due to leave Lampeter, we were missing a few Americans. I went to look for them and found them sitting on the kerb outside an eating place with a group of the people who had been eating there. With their Bibles open, they were telling the men about Jesus.

I always believed that my pastorate at Sandfields would not be a long one, perhaps five or six years. As it turned out it was seven-and-a-half years before I believed the Lord was opening the door for me to commence an itinerant ministry. This began in January 1994 when at a special meeting the Sandfields church set me apart for an itinerant ministry with Gospel Ministries.

I have often been asked what was it like to be pastor of the church in which Doctor Martyn Lloyd-Jones began his ministry. It was both great and problematic. It was a great privilege to follow on the great preachers who had been pastors at Sandfields since the Doctor. By any standards men like Emlyn Jones, John Thomas, Gwyn Williams and the others were powerful men in the pulpit. The problems arose from the church living in the past. What happened in the 1920s and 1930s when the Doctor was there was amazing and it is not difficult to see why they were days remembered with such great affection, but to live in the past is a deadly way of life for any church.

American team at Sandfields, 1993

I planted the seed, Apollos watered it, but God made it grow. So neither he who plants nor he who waters is anything, but only God, who makes things grow. The man who plants and the man who waters have one purpose, and each will be rewarded according to his own labour.

1 Corinthians 3:6-8

Salvation at Sandfields

NICOLA

In September 1986, I was a sixteen-year-old school girl, about to start in sixth-form college. I was brought up in a Christian family. My elder sister had become a Christian some years before and I think she somewhat despaired of my reluctance to consider Christianity as an option. I just did not want to think about it seriously at that time. The truth is, frankly, it was not 'cool' to be a Christian. The church where I was taken had few young people in it; my friends were at school, not church. I always believed there was a God and had heard the gospel so many times as I grew up, but it meant little to me. Church was boring.

In the summer of 1986, my sister, who was by now in university, suggested a trip to Greenbelt, a Christian Festival. While I was there, I heard about Christianity from a completely different perspective. I can remember little of the content now, but can vividly recall that there were hundreds of young people there—and they appeared to be quite normal human beings. In particular I was struck by my sister's Christian college friends. I mean no disrespect to the church when I say that, it's just that as a young person growing up in an ageing church, the people there, while in many cases being very lovely Christians, bore no resemblance to the type of people I went to school with, and had fun with.

In September 1986, Peter Jeffery came to my home church in Sandfields, Port Talbot. We had been without a minister for some time. On the Sunday night after he was inducted, he spoke on John 3:14 and 15: 'Just as Moses lifted up the snake in the desert, so the Son of Man must be lifted up, that everyone who believes in him may have eternal life.' Jesus compares himself in John 3 to the snake on the pole as the only way that we can survive the poison of sin which will kill us. I recall Peter Jeffery questioning what we would do if we were Israelites in the desert having been bitten by a snake, and what we would do in response. I remember thinking that if I was in the desert, I would be frantic to catch a glimpse of the snake on the pole. I imagined the Israelites jostling to see it. I felt I would have no choice but to look at Christ as my only salvation and the only way I would have life.

Life since then has not been straightforward, or even as I imagined it. My faith is stronger at some times than others, but I was recently reminded that, thankfully, my salvation does not rely on how strong or weak my faith is, but on a faithful, unchanging God who loves me.

ROB

I had from an early age an awareness of God, but it was very vague and I never went to any kind of church.

I began to work with a born-again Christian and in my eyes he was a 'decent' man, someone whose company everyone enjoyed. He explained in simple language that he had come to the point where he knew enough of the Bible through good church teaching, and watching his Christian parents and listening to them talk about matters of  faith (both things I never had), to realize that God was real and so was heaven and hell. He went on to explain to me that he realized at a very early stage that he could never meet the high standards God required of him to get to heaven and that he was bound for hell when he died. This shocked me as, in my eyes, if anyone deserved to go to heaven it was this really 'decent' guy. Then he told me the same fate awaited me!

I told my wife about this and we agreed to try to attend his church to hear for ourselves more of this gospel about Jesus and to hear about how his life affected ours. We attended fairly regularly and various things started to fall in to place. I began to pray to God, asking questions and being honest in these prayers explaining that I was both confused and a little scared with the full implication of the truth of this gospel. Unknown to me, God was also working in my wife's life to the point that she became a Christian before I did.

We were still attending my friend's church (at this point several people in his church had been praying for us both for many months), when my wife found out that there was a mums' and tots' club being run in a church just around the corner from us. She started to attend this and soon became friends with the women there.

One Sunday after returning home from work (we travelled twelve miles to attend my friend's church), she announced that we were going to try this local church that night.

By this point I knew I needed to be born again or 'saved' as I later heard it called, but no matter how hard I prayed nothing was happening and I knew that if I died then I would not go to heaven. We arrived at the service and immediately I stepped into the building I had an overwhelming sense that that night was going to be different and that made me really excited.

The pastor (Peter Jeffery) got into the pulpit and started to preach a sermon on Genesis 3—the 'fall of man' and redemption through the cross. I experienced something that I know has been repeated many times in many churches. As far as I was concerned, the preacher was delivering his message just to me and to nobody else. There was no sense of it being for anyone else in that church that night. There were many things said that seemed to just highlight what had been going on for the past eighteen months. When the sermon had ended, he encouraged all the people who felt God calling them to respond and turn to God.

I prayed for God to forgive my sins through his son Jesus, and I realized and accepted that Jesus died to take MY punishment for all that I had had done wrong, and would STILL do wrong, this side of death. I had a strong sense of being changed. I KNEW THAT I WAS SAFE.

ANDREW

I was raised in a loving Roman Catholic family. However, my opinion of the Catholic Church wavered greatly as I grew up. After a few years I even became an Altar boy. But as I grew more aware of the world, I even left that behind. I qualified as an electrician at a local car components factory at the age of twenty. The wage was good and I couldn't wait to spend it on enjoying myself. Then I met a girl!

This girl was different. We got on amazingly well. Her family was very 'religious', I had been told, but after getting to know them, I found them to be a caring and loving family. They didn't boast about their way of life. They just lived their lives for God and were always prepared to listen to and help anyone. I was convicted by their attitude and their love of God and church life, so much so that I even went back to Mass myself. This caused a few problems but, as our relationship deepened, Helen and I agreed to attend each other's church every Sunday. What a difference! The ritual of the Catholic Mass could not compare with the gospel set before me. The first service I attended was an unforgettable experience.

The years went by. We got married and hoped to start a family, etc. But things didn't turn out as we'd planned. We found having children difficult and lots of fertility treatment and treatment for illness began to take its toll on us. I stopped going to church. After my thirtieth birthday, I started feeling restless about my life, our marriage and my job. The future wasn't so certain anymore. I had rejected the Catholic Church for a new, livelier form of religion. But I was feeling dead inside. I was beginning to look for anything that would take away the loneliness and desperation I felt but could talk to no one about. That wasn't what men did, I thought. But a thought  popped into my head. Why not go to church again? So I went back every Sunday evening just before Christmas 1993. Peter Jeffery—he had married Helen and me seven years previously—was preaching, and I found myself soaking up every word I heard.

Every week my life seemed to come down to an hour or so on Sunday evening. I knew that I needed Jesus in my life or I would never have peace. Worst of all, hell would await me! I cried out in my mind for forgiveness, hoping for an answer week after week, but nothing happened—that is, until one night Helen looked at me on returning from church and saw the worry on my face. She suggested that I talk to her dad who, in turn, suggested I talk to Peter. That night I openly called on Jesus to have mercy on me. Even then the words faltered as I said them. I still felt no different. I determined then to read all I could about God, but had no peace of mind for weeks. During a holiday I almost drove Helen insane with my doubts, but on returning to church afterwards, we sang an old hymn called 'Man of Sorrows'. One line stood out. '"It is finished," was His cry.' What I had been waiting for had already been done. I just had to believe it and have faith in what Jesus had promised to all who call on his name for forgiveness.

I felt God's presence then and there. I finally knew the peace I longed for. I sat down and wept for joy.

Australia, 1994

Gospel ministries 1994, and facing poor health

Gospel Ministries was set up to facilitate my preaching and writing. A group of five fine young Christians organized it and I was free to do what I believed I did best—preach and write.

It only lasted one year before I experienced my second heart attack in January 1995 which forced me into early retirement at the age of fifty-seven years. But it was a busy year because, as well as preaching all over England and Wales, I had a preaching tour to Australia and three to North America. Future visits to these places as well as South Africa were lined up, but the Lord had other purposes.

I really enjoyed that year of itinerant ministry and felt that my preaching was beginning to know again something of the power of those days in Rugby. There were converts in Wales, England, Australia and the USA and there is nothing more thrilling and humbling than to see the Lord use one's preaching to bring souls to Christ. Why it should all finish after a year I do not know, but I have learnt that in the Christian life there is no such thing as bad luck. God is in control of all things. Sometimes it is difficult for us to appreciate this and with our limited vision we cannot make sense out of certain events. Often after a while we can look back and see why things happened as they did, but there are also events that we will never fully understand this side of heaven.

As I look back on fifty years of preaching, I have no complaints against God. I have done things, seen things, and been places that would never have been possible apart from the providential grace of God. So in January 1995, I started my enforced retirement wondering what God had in the future for me. To be honest I did not expect many more years. I was fifty-seven and with all my heart problems I never expected to reach the age of sixty. But that was nearly thirteen years ago and I have still been able to preach from time to time, even though at one point it was only one sermon a Sunday and now has had to be discontinued; books have been written and three are still scheduled to be published in the coming year. Since retirement, I have made several trips to the USA to preach, but my health now will probably not allow any more.

LIVING WITH POOR HEALTH

One of the most significant factors of my ministry since 1984 has been my poor health. This has governed to a degree what I have been able to do and not able to do. Up to this point, I had never been in hospital and had rarely been ill. I had only lost two weeks' preaching through illness and that was when I had a bad dose of 'flu'. But in 1984, everything changed. I had two operations and the following year I had my first heart attack. From then on, I have been in hospital at some point nearly every year—in fact, in all I have been in ten hospitals. I was feeling very pleased with myself when 2007 came to an end and, for the first time in many years I went a whole calendar year without having to be hospitalized. Then I came down to earth with a bump when in January 2008 I was back in again.

All this has obviously had an effect upon my ministry, the main one being in 1995 when my cardiologist told me that I had to retire from full-time work after I had my second heart attack. This came three years after I had had a quadruple heart bypass operation and the news came as rather a shock. I did not want to retire and felt I had a few sermons left in me yet. In fact, all that retirement meant was that I did not do any more pastoral visitation; the preaching and writing went on much as before.

The problem was that the condition of my heart and the medication I had to take every day was slowing me down considerably. But I am running ahead of the story a little. An angiogram in September 1991 showed that I had a serious heart condition and that I needed surgery. Heart problems in Wales are common and the waiting list for surgery is huge. The surgeon told me I was ninety-fifth on his list and that he was doing two operations a week. So I decided to preach right up to the time I was to go into hospital. That only lasted a couple of weeks because I was taken ill in the pulpit at Sandfields and finished up in intensive care. So I had no alternative but to sit it out until the following January when I had the bypass surgery.

During those months, I was only able to attend church on Sunday mornings. Like most preachers, I did not have the opportunity of hearing many preachers. Usually we only hear the best at conferences but now I was hearing all sorts of men. They all preached the truth but some were so long and most were simply boring. There were good ones but they were the exceptions. As I listened to these men I determined that, when I could preach again, I would preach shorter messages and never want to leave my congregation longing for me to stop. I was particularly disappointed with the students from college who were preparing for the ministry. They all preached far too long and appeared to be giving us the content of their past weeks' lectures at college.

I was relieved when at last I had the operation in January. A heart bypass operation is no small thing and, when I came round from the anaesthetic, there were so many tubes sticking out of me and I was so sore that I wondered why I had bothered! But within a couple of days I was much better and out of hospital in a week. I was amazed at how good I felt and I was preaching again within three months. As far as I was concerned, all my stays in hospital and all my operations were for one reason—to get me back into the pulpit.

In January 1995, I had a second heart attack and I realized that my heart condition was not going to go away. The third attack came in August 2005 and confirmed the problem. The cardiologist told me then that I could not have another bypass because I would not survive it. Apparently I only have one good artery working.

My condition at present is that I get so tired and breathless that everything is an effort to do. I have not preached for nearly a year and don't get to church very often. But I started preaching when I was eighteen years old and am now seventy, so there is little to complain about!

Poor health is obviously not pleasant to live with, but it is no excuse for idleness. I think we have to work within the limits God puts upon us and those limits can be very flexible. After my first heart attack, family and friends made the point to me that I was doing too much and needed to cut back. Such talk is good for the ego but one has to be wary of it. During one Sunday in hospital, I decided to read Ecclesiastes and was reminded again of verse 10 of chapter 9: 'Whatever your hand finds to do, do it with all your might.'

Your might may not be as much as it used to be, but still you work for God with nothing held back. One old preacher put it like this: 'It is better to burn out for God than to rust out.'

Dr Martyn Lloyd-Jones

Influences

I never heard a sermon until I was over seventeen years old. When I started my courtship with Lorna, she took me along to her church, the Green Mission on Neath. It was a small church with a lay pastor. Ben Rosser was an engineer in a local factory and he was an excellent preacher. He was the first preacher I heard. Pastor Rosser was meticulous in his handling of Scripture and preached with vigour and animation. When I started to preach, I think something of his style rubbed off on me and I have never regretted that.

It was in the Green Mission that I preached first, did my first children's meeting and soon was organizing the Sunday School. The folk there were keen, enthusiastic and committed and this also served as a good example to me.

When I received the call to the ministry, Lorna and I knew what God wanted from us but we did not know what the next step should be. We belonged to a small mission hall that had no denominational connections, so we turned for advice to a friend of Pastor Rosser, Pastor Luther Rees, who was the minister of a congregational church in Llansamlet, some four miles from us. Pastor Rees was a tremendous help and arranged for me to enter the Congregational College in Swansea. His son, Neville, was already a student there. I have never known ministers like Luther and Neville Rees who exercised such a faithful and consistent pastoral visitation ministry as these two. I never felt that the pastoral side of the work was very strong in my ministry but looking at these two kept me at it.

In the late 1950s, God called a good group of young men in South Wales into the ministry. Some were in the Presbyterian college in Aberystwyth, some in the Baptist college in Cardiff and others in the Congregational college in Swansea. We were all doing the same University of Wales course in theology, which meant that we had very little biblical theology. To make up for this, Luther Rees and a friend of his, Rev I B Davies, organized occasional Saturdays for us to get together for ministry. These were blessed days and greatly appreciated.

Rev Elwyn Davies was secretary of the Evangelical Movement of Wales and a man highly respected by evangelicals. He was a great encouragement to me. It was his enthusiasm that saw my first book, *All Things New*, published. Elwyn was the instigator of the first trip overseas to preach. Throughout my ministry, whenever I had a difficult pastoral problem, it was to Elwyn that I turned for advice. I even sent Christian couples with marriage problems to see him.

The greatest influence upon my preaching was that of Dr Martyn Lloyd-Jones. The first books of his that I read were the two volumes on the Sermon on the Mount. After that, I could not get enough books by the Doctor. He preached at my induction to the church at Rugby and, on several occasions, spent a week on a farm belonging to some of our members. I was always invited to go for tea one day of the week and to spend a couple of hours alone with the Doctor. This was an enormous privilege and one I highly valued.

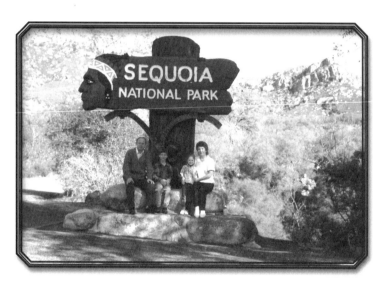

**In the Sequoia National Park,
California**

Overseas preaching

I first preached overseas in 1982. I received an invitation from Tullarmarine Baptist Church in Melbourne, Australia, to go and help them for a few weeks. They had recently moved doctrinally to a position which recognized and appreciated the historic, reformed faith, and I spent seven weeks preaching there. This was a small church and, though the people were willing to pay my airfare, they would not be able to afford a salary. This was taken care of by my church in Rugby who continued to pay my salary while I was away.

I made that journey on my own but some folk in the Melbourne church invited me and my family to be their guests for a couple of weeks over Christmas 1983. The girls were unable to come, but Lorna, David and I went. All expenses were paid and we had a glorious time with them. This was primarily a holiday but I also did some preaching.

I was in Australia again in 1986 and 1994. The visit in 1986 was booked for two months' preaching in February and March, but I had a heart attack the previous August and, for a while, the it was not certain that the trip would come about. But I was determined to go and suffered no ill effect from the effort.

I am aware that I speak very quickly when I preach and this, coupled with my Welsh accent, could be a problem outside of Wales. In fact at the beginning of the 1982 trip, I overheard two Aussies saying of me, 'We brought this bloke half way around the world to preach to us and we can't understand a word he is saying!' Thankfully, that was not the general view and God richly blessed the preaching.

Only once have I had a problem getting myself understood. I was preaching at a conference in Pennsylvania, USA, and I had a bad cold which was affecting my voice. I was conscious that I was not getting through to the listeners and this was confirmed at the end of the week when an elderly man said to me, 'I understand that you are a good preacher but I have not understood a word you have said all week.' There is no answer to that!

On one of the flights to Australia, I was telling the man sitting next to me the reason for my trip. He replied that the Australians

Australia with Lorna and David, 1993

would not listen to me because all they were interested in was sport and pleasure. But I found the Aussies to be warm and friendly. They loved the Word of God and listened intently to the preaching. We never had great numbers at the meetings but a series of sermons I preached in the evenings at the Melbourne Institute of Biblical Studies on the subject of revival saw us change rooms a few times as more and more people attended.

The church at Rugby supported the ministry of a small church in Spain and every tenth Sunday, the whole collection went to this work. Several times I went to Spain to preach. The first time I was terrified at the thought of preaching through a translator. Would I be able to speak in short sentences, stopping every minute or so? But the Spanish pastor who did the translation was superb and I never had the slightest problem—that is, except on one occasion. He was so overwhelmed emotionally by what we were saying that he dissolved into tears and disappeared out of the pulpit. An English missionary took his place, but after a few minutes, the same thing happened to him and there I was, left alone

Spain, 1992

in the pulpit in front of the Spanish congregation, not knowing what to do. Thankfully a member of the congregation came to my rescue by closing the meeting in prayer.

My first trip to the USA was in 1992 and in all I made about fifteen preaching tours there. I loved preaching in America. I know that the Americans have a reputation for being shallow and that American evangelicalism has been discourteously described as being 'three thousand miles wide and half an inch deep'. But my experience was that the churches I preached at, and the believers I met, were in a different league from those in the UK. The enthusiasm and commitment was a joy to see and experience. In all I preached in ten states and at about thirty different churches.

Arizona, 1994

There were some memorable trips to America. One was to preach in 1996 at the Mid America Reformed Baptist Conference in Indiana. I was one of three speakers who preached each day to the nine hundred people present. The organizers particularly asked me to preach the gospel each day. The Lord blessed the four sermons in quite a remarkable way. I left the conference believing that up to twenty people had been converted, but I later learnt that the number was nearer forty. It was truly an amazing week.

On our first visit to California, Lorna and I were met in San Francisco by one of the pastors of the church in Visalia where I was going to preach for a week. Before driving inland to Visalia, Pastor Jeff, who was hosting us, took us down the lovely California coast to Monterey. We were to have lunch there and Pastor Jeff said that the church insisted that we eat in the best restaurant in town and I was to choose the place. We drove around looking for somewhere when I spotted the place I wanted to eat at—Kentucky Fried Chicken. Jeff was amazed at the place I had chosen, but KFC was just what I wanted.

Preaching in California was a whole new experience for me. The culture is so different from South Wales and it shows in the style of people's worship. The preacher is clapped into the pulpit and applauded again at the end of the sermon!

It was on this trip to the USA that I fully began to realize that many things we do in church life are cultural or local traditions. For instance, on the east coast I preached at several churches where the congregation stand for the Bible reading. I had never seen that before but it was all part of how these folk worshipped.

With the Gaydosh family at the top of the Empire State Building

In the year of Gospel Ministries, 1994, I did my longest tour. Starting at El Paso in Texas, we then went to Albuquerque in New Mexico. We then moved across to Camp Verde in Arizona and this was followed by a long drive across the desert to Los Angeles. In all we drove about five thousand miles and I preached fifty times in six weeks. Every time I preached evangelistically, there were converts. It was exhausting, exhilarating and thrilling.

One day, the folk who were organizing my itinerary told me that the church I was due at the following Sunday had cancelled the meeting. They said they would try and find somewhere else for me to preach. The substitute they came up with was the Grace Community Church where Dr John MacArthur is the pastor-teacher. This was the biggest church I have ever preached at. There were two morning services with 2,000 at the first and 3,000 at the second. They asked me to preach the same sermon at both services and the Lord enabled me to preach with great liberty from Romans 5:1.

I first received invitations to preach in North America because churches there had been using my books. In fact more are sold there than in Britain. On my first trip, we had a meal with a family where the wife had been converted through reading my book *Seeking God*. She told me that her neighbour had also been saved through reading this book. This church on Long Island, where Mike Gaydosh was the pastor, was to be our base for several more visits on the east coast.

Most of the American churches I preached at did little evangelistic preaching—perhaps only once every couple of months—but many people were saved. This was because of the enthusiasm of the believers in the churches. At one church in California, I was introduced to a lady who had been saved through listening to a tape-recorded message of my preaching. She was keen for me to preach in her home so that she could invite all her neighbours. I preached to about seventy people in her home and almost a half of them were unbelievers.

Peter with American ladies

Sandfields bookstall in market

13 Writing books

It has always seemed to me a most amazing thing that I of all people should write a book. I was an only child and when my father died, I felt I ought to leave school to earn some money for my mother and me. So, at the age of fifteen, I left school with no academic qualifications whatsoever, and started work in a factory.

The books began as a result of the blessings God was giving us in the church at Rugby. We were having many converts and I wanted a book to give them that would help at the beginning of their Christian life. As far as I knew there was nothing suitable available so I wrote *All Things New*. That was in 1976 and many years and some 60,000 copies later, it is still being of some use to new converts. Since then, over forty books have been written and some translated into Russian, Chinese, Italian. Spanish, Swedish, Romanian, Arabic and Welsh.

Some folk have been kind enough to say that I have the gift of being able to present difficult concepts simply. I don't know about that, but I write as I preach, and in preparing for both, I am always asking myself this question: will the people be able to understand this? This seems to me to be the obvious question to ask, and, if I can achieve this, I will be putting the cookies—the rich teaching of the Word of God—within the reach of ordinary people. Preaching or writing that fails to do so is a futile exercise.

My first small booklet, *All Things New*, was intended for the use of the converts we were having in Rugby and was produced first of all as a duplicated booklet. It was for our own use and was not meant for anyone else, but one thing led to another and it was published in 1976. Originally written based on the Authorized (King James) Version, it has been reprinted in 2008 on a new format and this time based on the text of the NIV.

Other books then followed at the rate of about one a year. Most of them were small books because I have a theory that many Christians rarely read books of more than a hundred pages, so I wrote books they could start and finish without too much effort. Of the earliest books—I think my favourite—was *Stand Firm—a young Christian's guide to the armour of God*. In the introduction to this book I wrote:

'COME to Jesus, and all your problems will be over is the message we hear from some preachers. Certain hymns, too, seem to confirm this teaching— like the chorus that ends, 'And now I am happy all the day.' Unfortunately, however, that is not the Christian's experience after conversion and, more importantly, that is not what the Scriptures teach.

When a person comes to Christ in repentance and faith, sin—his greatest problem—is dealt with. The joy of salvation and the experience of peace with God can be overwhelming, and with some this may last for days, weeks or even months. But eventually other problems, completely unknown in pre-conversion days, will begin to make themselves felt. As a result, far from being 'happy all the day', the young Christian will know the misery of doubts, guilt and conviction of sin as never before. On top of all this, he will have to face misunderstanding and opposition to his new-found faith from friends and relatives.

All this can seem quite devastating to the new convert, but the Scriptures assure us that it is only to be expected. The Lord Jesus himself said to his disciples, 'In the world you will have trouble' (John 16:33). And the apostle Paul, returning to churches which he had established on his first missionary journey to strengthen and encourage them, told them, 'We must go through many hardships to enter the kingdom of God' (Acts 14:22).

Why should it be like this? The fact is that when we become Christians, we enter not a holiday camp where everything is jolly and comfortable, but rather a battle station in the middle of a fierce war. We are now soldiers in the Lord's army, and the enemy exerts tremendous pressure upon us. How we fare in this spiritual battle depends to a great extent upon how we are equipped.

In many ways the sentiments expressed there lie behind all my books. Many of them are written for young believers to instruct and encourage them in their new spiritual life. In 1988, the *Christian Handbook* was published which is a straightforward guide to the Bible, church history and Christian doctrine. There I tried to be brief, simple and accurate in presenting information (in just two hundred pages) that would normally only be available in larger and more expensive volumes.

That there is a need for this sort of book as has been illustrated by the popularity of another small volume, *Bite-sized Theology*. This is an ABC of the Christian faith and is simply a book of basic Bible doctrine. It was published in 2000 and has been reprinted every year since.

Nearly all my books started off as sermons and then were developed into book form. Three exceptions to this are my ventures into Church history. The latest, *Preachers who made a difference*, is a brief history of some of the great preachers of the past and to give some idea of their preaching the publishers have included with the book a CD on which I read extracts from their sermons. Needless to say, there were no cassette recorders in the days of J C Ryle and Robert Murray M'Cheyne!

A note to readers: A full list of Peter Jeffery's books is to be found in Appendix 3 on page 114.

News of this reached the ears of the church at Jerusalem, and they sent Barnabas to Antioch. When he arrived and saw the evidence of the grace of God, he was glad and encouraged them all to remain true to the Lord with all their hearts. He was a good man, full of the Holy Spirit and faith, and a great number of people were brought to the Lord. Then Barnabas went to Tarsus to look for Saul, and when he found him, he brought him to Antioch. So for a whole year Barnabas and Saul met with the church and taught great numbers of people. The disciples were called Christians first at Antioch.

Acts 11:22-25

What is a true conversion?

Like all preachers, I have had the sad experience of seeing people making a profession of faith only for them to fall away in a few weeks or months. It is obvious by then that they were never saved. No one wants this, but how can it be avoided? What is a true conversion? Are we making two basic errors in our evangelism? Are we, on the one hand, making salvation seem too difficult, and on the other hand, making it seem too easy?

We make it too difficult with a wrong understanding of the sovereignty of God in salvation. It is true that only God can save, but that does not remove a person's responsibility to seek the Lord. Do we encourage sinners to seek the Lord? Do we preach for this?

Then we make it too easy with a glib 'easy believism' which removes conviction and repentance and makes salvation a simple nod of approval on the sinner's part. It is this that produces the false professions of faith.

The fruit of evangelism is saved souls. But how are we to know if someone is genuinely converted? Warren Wiersbe makes the strong point that 'There is a difference between "fruit" and "results". You can get "results" by following sure-fire formulas, manipulating people, or turning on your charisma; but "fruit" comes from life. When the Spirit of life is working through the Word of life, the seed planted bears fruit; and that fruit has in it the seeds for more fruit (Genesis 1:11–12). Results are counted and soon become silent statistics, but living fruit remains and continues to multiply to the glory of God (John 15:6).'

It is obvious both from the New Testament and our own experience that not all who profess faith in Christ are truly converted. In Acts 8 we are told of a man who believed and was baptized. Yet soon after, the apostle Peter tells him that his heart is not right before God and that he is full of bitterness and captive to sin. Earlier in the New Testament, in his parable of the sower, the Lord Jesus himself had warned of the possibility of false professions. Some people receive the gospel warmly but they last only a short time because there is no root in them, that is, no real experience of Christ (Mark 4:17).

A SERIOUS PROBLEM

False profession of faith is a very serious problem. It is serious for the people who make a profession of faith that is not real. They may be told they are Christians but it is soon obvious that they are not. Often such people become so disillusioned with the Christian faith that they become almost impossible to reach with further evangelism. Several years ago, I was preaching in an open-air meeting in the local market. All the time our meeting was going on a young man stood nearby selling Communist Workers' newspapers. After we had finished I went to speak to him and during our conversation he firmly told me that Christianity was a fraud, because it did not work. He was convinced of this, he said, because he had once been a Christian. He had been 'saved' by going forward at a large crusade meeting and he had a decision card to prove it. But after a short time he realized, so he said, that he had been deceived. Becoming a Christian (as he thought) had changed nothing in his life so he had become a Communist instead.

Nothing I could say to him touched him. He was hard and unyielding in his opposition to the gospel.

It is also serious for the church, which may be thanking God in prayer and praise for a person's supposed conversion one day, only to find that within a short time the 'new convert' is back in the world and rarely if ever seen in church. This sort of experience can easily demoralize and discourage believers in their evangelistic efforts.

It is serious, too, for nominal Christians, those good churchgoers who are always in church but have never been saved. They are actually encouraged in their nominalism when they see false professions. What happens is this: someone in the church is claimed to have been saved. He or she is encouraged to give a testimony but, before long, stops attending the Sunday services. The nominal Christian sees this as showing how meaningless is all this business of being saved. He or she says, 'I have never had a saving experience but am still in church, unlike so-and-so.'

A SOLUTION

False professions of faith are a serious problem in all sorts of ways, but the worst thing about them is that they bring dishonour to the name of God. So how do we solve this problem?

First of all, we must acknowledge that the problem will never disappear altogether. If it occurred during the revival in Samaria described in Acts 8, it will also occur in our less spiritually enlightened days: That is a fact but it is no excuse for indifference. We must try to reduce drastically the number of times it happens.

One way to do this is to examine biblically our methods of evangelism. If we substitute an 'easy believism' which only requires an intellectual agreement with certain gospel truths and ignores the New Testament demand for repentance and faith, then shallow, superficial 'conversions' will abound. The decision system practised in much modern evangelicalism aggravates the problem. For many people, this system, which was unknown until the early nineteenth century, has become an indispensable part of evangelism. Indeed, many people think that they become Christians merely by 'going forward' at an evangelistic meeting. To be fair, some evangelists are careful to say this is not so, but because of the widespread use of the practice, people still think it is the only way to be saved. (For a more detailed study on this subject see the little booklet, *The Invitation System* by Iain Murray, published by the Banner of Truth Trust.)

In recent years, amazing claims have been made of the thousands who are alleged to be saved through mass evangelism. Everyone knows that not all who go forward are truly converted, but it is argued that if only a fraction prove to be genuine, then the method is justified. I can understand the sentiments behind this argument, but the New Testament will not allow us to forget the others, namely those thousands who were wrongly told they were Christians, thought they really were Christians, but soon became disillusioned because, in reality, they were nothing of the kind. The damage is enormous and unnecessary. It is caused not by the gospel, but by a system of evangelism that has no biblical foundation. This kind of thing is not confined to mass evangelism. It also happens at summer camps and in local churches. How do we deal with it?

We should be more careful about publicly labelling a profession of faith as a conversion. Professions can be the result of several things: emotionalism, pressure from friends, sincere desires, or even just being deceived. True conversion is always and only produced by the convicting and regenerating work of the Holy Spirit, in which the gifts of repentance and faith are imparted to the soul.

Our spiritual forefathers used to make a distinction between a 'soul awakened' and a 'soul converted'. Profession of faith is sometimes the premature response of a heart that has been awakened to sin and its dangers. Of course, if God begins a work in someone's heart, he will surely bring it to completion. However, impatient for results, we may mistake mere concern or interest for the work of the Spirit, and so encourage a profession from one who is not regenerate.

In Acts 11 we see marks of true conversion.

1. THERE WAS A GREAT CHANGE IN THEIR LIVES

In Acts 11:23, Barnabas saw the grace of God made evident in people's lives. But grace is abstract and cannot be seen or touched, so what did he see? You cannot see electricity, but you can see the difference it makes when a light is switched on in a dark room, and if you touch a bare wire you will feel its power. So it is with the grace of God. There was a difference in the people Barnabas met and a power in their lives that had not been there before. 'If anyone is in Christ,' Paul tells the Corinthians, 'he is a new creation; the old has gone, the new has come!' (2 Corinthians 5:17).

When a person is converted certain things change. Some happen immediately and some gradually, but either way there will be a change. It is bound to happen. John Newton continued in the slave trade for a time after he was saved, but eventually fought for its abolition. Desires, ambitions and longings all change. Matthew Henry makes the point that if your 'salvation' has done nothing for your temper, then clearly it has done nothing for your soul.

2. THEY LOVED THE LORD JESUS CHRIST

In Acts 11:26, we read that the disciples were called Christians for the first time at Antioch. This was not a title they took upon themselves but was originally a name of scorn given to believers by the world. However, it demonstrates that unbelievers saw something in them, and heard things from them, that could only be explained by their new relationship to Christ. People who once worshipped idols with them, got drunk with them and cursed with them were now renouncing all these things and talking about their love for Christ. So they were called 'Christians'. Love for Christ is a prime evidence of grace, and if anyone does not give evidence his new affection, we have no right to call such a person a Christian, whatever he or she professes to believe doctrinally. Of this love John writes, 'We love [him] because he first loved us' (1 John 4:19). Anyone who does not love Christ has not understood the love of Christ for sinners, and cannot therefore be a believer.

3. THEY LOVED THE WORD OF GOD

These new believers were teachable and had a hunger for Scripture. So they submitted themselves willingly to the things taught by Paul and Barnabas. Spiritually newborn babes 'crave pure spiritual milk' so that by it they may grow up in their salvation (see 1 Peter 2:2). Why should they have this desire? Because the Scriptures testify to Christ and reveal him both in his glorious person and his saving work. Those who love Christ will also love his Word, the Bible.

4. THEY LOVED ONE ANOTHER

The believers met together as a church, not because it was a rule but a desire. All true Christians love fellowship in the gospel with their fellow-believers (Philippians 1:5) and will always seek it out. It is also clear in Acts 11:29 that they even had love for Christians they had never met. A new convert does not have to be coaxed to go to church: such a person longs to join with other believers in the worship of God and the service of Christ.

5. THEY LOVED THE LOST

In Acts 11:24 we read that a great number believed and came to Christ. This was after the initial blessing of verse 21, and came about through the ministry of Barnabas. But it was also, no doubt, the result of the converts' concern for others. The new Christians were not slow to evangelize.

These, then, are some of the evidences of grace we look to look for when someone makes a profession of faith. But remember we are dealing with newborn babes and the evidence will not always be there in a fully-fledged way. When dealing with tender new life, we must guard against being naïve and gullible on one hand, and too critical on the other. It is fruit we want to see, not mere results. Results may bring praise to us but only fruit will bring glory to the Lord.

Baglan CD sample

Postscript

I retired from full-time work in 1995, but since then I have preached regularly, at least until recently. I still write books and, in recent years, I have started producing CDs and DVDs of some of my old sermons. A friend who lives in New York gave me an Apple computer with a built in camera. This has enabled me to produce a series of 'The Gospel in Five Minutes' DVDs on such subjects as, 'Why you need to become a Christian', 'Who wants to be a millionaire?', 'Who wants a Rolex?' etc. These can be seen on my web site, <www.peterjeffery.org.uk>.

In September 2002, three young men who had been converted when I was at Sandfields started a new church on the estate where my wife and I live. Since then, Baglan Community Church has flourished, and up to 150 people can be present on a Sunday morning. Lorna and I are now members there.

The greatest burden of my heart all through my ministry has been to see souls saved, and I urge all believers to share this burden. Whether preaching from a pulpit, or sharing the gospel in a one-to-one situation, it is an unspeakable privilege to tell men and women, dead in their sins, about God's love in Christ, a mighty Saviour whose name is 'Wonderful, Counsellor, Mighty God, Everlasting Father, Prince of Peace' (Isaiah 9:6). It is our privilege to tell them of the glory of the incarnation, of the beauty of his sinless life, of the death he died to redeem us, of divine justice satisfied, and of the resurrection, ascension and exaltation of Christ; and also to tell them that God demands a response, namely, that we should repent of our sins and come in faith to Christ.

What a joy and privilege to speak of these things! And what joy it is to see the Holy Spirit working in the hearts of sinners—to see indifference and apathy turn to concern, concern to conviction, and then conviction to salvation. There is nothing like it! To be a soul-winner makes you feel ten feet tall, but at the same time it makes you feel like dust. It is humbling to realize that God condescends to use a sinner like you, with all your faults, to save another soul. Your joy is such that you want to see more souls saved. And there is only one thing that will save sinners—the gospel of Jesus Christ. So you want to tell it with more faithfulness, greater love, greater urgency and greater power. You want success—not just because it makes you feel good, but because God is glorified and sinners are saved from hell.

The soul-winner is a person with a great longing to see God glorified in the salvation of sinners. The difficulties and problems of witness do not put him off; they serve only to enhance his sense of urgency and drive him to the Lord in earnest prayer.

True Preaching

Preaching should confront men and women with God and eternity. In order to do this, it has to be biblical. It has to tell people what God is saying in his Word. From the preacher's point of view, this does two things. It helps to give him an authority that is far more than his own ability and gifts of oratory. People need to know that God is speaking through his servant. Secondly, it gives the preacher an endless source of material to preach. He is not dependent upon current events for his sermon topics, but has a huge reservoir of biblical teaching to draw upon.

Great preachers varied in nationality, temperament and sometimes in doctrine but they all sought to bring God to the people. This is why they made a difference. They set out not merely to inform people, but to transform them. The most drastic and radical transformation that a man can know is that from spiritual death to spiritual life. These men preached for this. They knew that the sinner's greatest need is for regeneration so they preached to reach his heart and soul. This governed how they preached and created in them a great desire to preach Christ, the cross and his redeeming blood.

They preached to create a conviction of sin in the unbeliever. It is not conviction of sin for a man to feel bad because he is drinking too much or generally making a mess of his life. Sin is not just a violation of socially accepted standards. To see sin only in social or moral terms will not lead people to conviction. Sin must be seen in the light of the law and holiness of God. The gospel is not an aspirin for the aches of life, to soothe and comfort people in their misery. It is a holy God's answer to the violation of divine law by human beings whose very nature is to rebel against him.

Most people think salvation is the product of morality and religious observance. In spite of the clarity of the New Testament message, they still cling to their own efforts to save themselves. But salvation by works never creates conviction of sin because it fails miserably to take into account the holiness, purity and justice of God. It sees sin only as a moral or social blemish and not as an affront to the Word, law and character of God. It is the law of God which produces conviction because it shows us our sin in relationship, not to society and people, but to God. It shows us that we have failed to meet God's requirements.

A common feature of all great preachers is a longing for success—to see souls saved. Andrew Bonar says of Robert Murray M'Cheyne, 'He entertained so full a persuasion that a faithful minister has every reason to expect to see souls converted under him, that when this was withheld, he began to fear that some hidden evil was provoking the Lord and grieving the Spirit. And ought it not to be so with all of us? Ought we not to suspect, either that we are not living near to God, or that our message is not a true transcript of the glad tidings, in both matter and manner, when we see no souls brought to Jesus?'[1]

Bonar continues. 'Two things he seems never to have ceased from—the cultivation of personal holiness and the most anxious efforts to win souls.'[2] How M'Cheyne links these two things is highly significant. He wrote to William Burns in September 1840, 'I am also deepened in my conviction, that if we are to be instruments in such a work, we must be purified from all filthiness of the flesh and spirit. Oh, cry for personal holiness, constant nearness to God, by the blood of the Lamb. Bask in his beams—lie back in the arms of love—be filled with his Spirit—or all success in the ministry will only be to your own everlasting confusion ... How much more useful might we be, if we were only more free from pride, self conceit, personal vanity, or some secret sin that our heart knows. Oh! hateful sins, that destroy our peace and ruin souls.'[3]

M'Cheyne believed that 'In the case of a faithful ministry, success is the rule and the lack of it the exception.'[4] And when there was no success, no souls saved, he did not blame the people but looked first at his own heart.

BORN NOT MADE

Preachers are born, not made. Was Jeremiah the only preacher set apart by God before he was born (Jeremiah 1:5)? Was he an exception or the norm? Preachers are not the products of education and training but are men set apart by God and equipped by the Holy Spirit for their life's work. This does not mean that they do not need training, but above all there needs to be the call of God. Spurgeon, Lloyd-Jones and Moody had no formal theological training but it was obvious that they were prepared by God and that his hand was upon them. Preaching is a special gift from God and those who have it need to guard it carefully and seek to nurture it for use to God's glory.

Many evangelicals today have lost confidence in preaching. We may lament this and mourn the fact that in some churches music and drama have replaced preaching. But why has it happened? Is it not the fault of preachers themselves? Is it not because gospel preaching too often lacks authority, relevance and power, and consequently fails to save souls? It has been said that the most urgent need in the Christian church today is true preaching. Most preachers would agree with that but many Christians in the pew do not. That is not surprising if the preaching they hear is so sentimental as to have no substance, or so intellectual that they cannot understand it.

What is true preaching? What constitutes true gospel preaching? It involves both a proper content and a correct presentation. The gospel must be preached in a language that people can understand. In the last century, Spurgeon was pleading, 'We need in the ministry, now and in all time, men of plain speech. The preacher's language must not be that of the classroom, but of all classes; not of the university, but of the universe … "Use market language," said George Whitefield, and we know the result. We need men who not only speak so that they can be understood, but so that they cannot be misunderstood.'[5] Plain speech is not slang but simple language and concepts that people can understand.

Preachers will only make a difference when their preaching clearly shows to people the Lord Jesus Christ. The only difference that is of any significance is the one Christ makes in the hearts of men and women. It is possible for a preacher to make a difference to his hearers that is only temporary. He comes and preaches and makes a great impact but if you passed that way in a year's time, you would see that there is now no longer any difference to be seen. It was only temporary and this is because it was not the gospel, not Christ, that made the difference but the preacher himself. Such preaching is only a form of entertainment. It does not confront sinners with God, but merely holds their attention for a while until something else comes along.

Appendix 1

A SERIOUS RESPONSIBILITY

Preaching is not a hobby but should occupy a man's whole life and thinking. The preacher sees everything in relationship to his ministry. In this sense he is never on holiday. His mind is continuously taken up with the next sermon and the next congregation. The seriousness of the matter causes what Paul calls in 1 Corinthians 2:3–4 a 'trembling'. What do we know of this trembling? Why did Paul with all his great abilities preach in weakness, fear and trembling? Surely it must have been because he felt the awesome responsibility preaching puts upon a man.

Preachers who make a difference know something of this trembling. It was said of M'Cheyne that when he entered the pulpit, people would weep before he opened his mouth—to quote Lloyd-Jones, 'There was something about his face, and in the conviction which his hearers possessed that he had come from God; he was already preaching before he opened his mouth. A man sent from God is aware of this burden. He trembles because of the momentous consequences, the issues, that depend upon what he does.'[6]

Preaching is the most exciting and uncertain activity a man can partake in. The preacher never knows what is going to happen when he steps into a pulpit. In fact, anything can happen when the power of the Holy Spirit comes and divine unction dominates the ministry. Thomas Olivers was antagonistic to the gospel and went to hear George Whitefield preach in the open air with the intention of disrupting the meeting. But when the preacher started, he was unable to interrupt and was compelled to listen. Whitefield had a bad turn in his eye and his enemies called him Dr Squintum, but Olivers said that it did not matter which way Whitefield's head was facing, 'his eye was always on me.' He was saved and went on to write that great hymn 'The God of Abraham praise'.

Preaching is also a battle because the devil hates it. He does not mind men who get into a pulpit to give a nice, gentle homily, but he hates it when Christ is uplifted and sinners are confronted with the holy God. This battle takes many forms. Sometimes it is in the heart and mind of the preacher as he grapples with his own unworthiness. Sometimes the devil attacks him before he leaves home for church with tensions with his children. Sometimes the attack is frontal. One of the greatest preachers I have ever heard was the late Douglas MacMillan of Scotland. Douglas was preaching for us at Rugby in a series of evangelistic meetings. I was ill in bed and unable to attend. After the service Douglas came into my bedroom to see me, and I could see by his face that the service had not gone well.

Some of the young men of the church had gone into the streets to try to get passers-by to come in. They persuaded two twelve-year-old boys to come. The boys came in and were quiet throughout the service but Douglas told me that he felt evil coming from one of these boys which bound him in his preaching. Douglas MacMillan was a strong man physically, intellectually and spiritually, yet this twelve-year-old boy so affected his preaching that he felt bound. That has to be the attack of Satan.

Preaching is no cosy chat but a taking on of hell in preaching the gospel to sinners. The best of sermons can be left flat and lifeless. The greatest sense of expectancy can be dashed. But the opposite is also true, and such power can come from God on to the preaching that is inexplicable in terms of anything merely human. Heaven and hell are locked in battle when the gospel is preached.

UNCTION

Great preachers are so only because God is pleased to bless their preaching and use them in remarkable ways. They will have other things going for them, such as natural abilities, but it is God who makes the difference. They are aware of this and are continuously sensitive to the hand of God on them. To them, this is the only thing that matters. They will prepare their sermons diligently and seek to prepare themselves spiritually, but they do not depend on these and all the time they look for divine unction.

Dr Lloyd-Jones once told a ministers' conference, 'You think my sermons come down from heaven each Saturday evening on a silver plate, but they don't. I have to work for them.' The Doctor was stressing the need for careful preparation of the sermon, but he also knew that there was more needed. He said, 'Seek Him! Seek Him! What can we do without Him? Seek Him! Seek Him always. But go beyond seeking Him; expect Him. Do you expect anything to happen when you get up to preach in a pulpit? Or do you just say to yourself, "Well, I have prepared my address, I am going to give them this address; some of them will appreciate it and some will not." Are you expecting it to be the turning point in someone's life? Are you expecting anyone to have a climactic experience? That is what preaching is meant to do. That is what you find in the Bible and in the subsequent history of the church. Seek this power, expect this power, yearn for this power; and when the power comes, yield to Him. Do not resist. Forget all about your sermon if necessary. Let Him loose you, let Him manifest His power in you and through you. I am certain, as I have said several times before, that nothing but a return of this power of the Spirit on our preaching is going to avail us anything. This makes true preaching, and it is the greatest need of all today—never more so. Nothing can substitute for this. But, given this, you will have a people who will be anxious and ready to be taught and instructed, and led ever further and more deeply into "the truth as it is in Christ Jesus". This "unction", this "anointing", is the supreme thing. Seek it until you have it; be content with nothing less. Go on until you can say, "And my speech and my preaching was not with enticing words of man's wisdom, but in demonstration of the Spirit and of power." He is still able to do "exceeding abundantly above all that we can ask or think".'[7]

The preacher needs God with him in the pulpit. He not only preaches about God but he wants also to experience the presence of God with him as he preaches. If he does not he will cease to make a difference. He may continue to be popular and to a degree be useful, but he will not be making the difference that matters.

REFERENCES

1 **Andrew Bonar,** *Memoirs & Remains*, Middleton, 1965, page 79

2 **Bonar,** page 150

3 **Bonar,** page 250

4 **Bonar,** page 250

5 **Charles Spurgeon,** *Banner of Truth Magazine*, April 1960

6 **D M Lloyd-Jones,** *Knowing the Times*, Banner of Truth, 1989

7 **D M Lloyd-Jones,** *Preachers and Preaching*, Hodder and Stoughton, page 325

❝ A Sermon: The most-hated teaching in the Bible

A world that can tolerate just about anything—homosexuality, lesbianism, abortion—cannot tolerate one way to God.

Of all things about the Christian faith what the world hates most is the teaching about the uniqueness and exclusiveness of Jesus.

Jesus said, 'The world … hates me' (John 7:7).

How can the world hate the most loving and gentle man who ever lived? How can it hate a Jesus so gracious, merciful, compassionate? Jesus tells us in the same verse in these words: 'Because I tell them they are evil.' It is because Jesus told them they were wrong and he was the only way to God. Their religion was wrong; their morals were wrong; their philosophy was wrong.

The world hates authority and particularly absolute authority that allows for no alternative. What is a philosopher? He is a man who tells you what he thinks. He has spent his whole adult life in or around universities; he has umpteen degrees; has written books and he tells us, 'This is what I think about God.' But what he thinks about God has no more worth that what a road sweeper thinks about God.

We need to hear what God has to say. We have to look to the Bible. But the world hates the Bible because it teaches us only one way to God. From beginning to end it does this. The one way is always God's way.

I WANT TO SHOW YOU THAT THE ONLY WAY TO GOD IS JESUS, AND THAT THIS IS REASONABLE.

A young woman in her mid-twenties came into the church one Sunday for the first time. After the service I spoke to her and discovered she was a school teacher and a very devout Roman Catholic. 'If you are a Roman Catholic,' I said, 'why have you come to an evangelical church?' She answered, 'I know God but I know nothing about Jesus. I want to learn about Jesus.' I replied, 'You cannot know God without Jesus.' She was amazed at the answer, as many religious people would be, but the Bible is very clear that Jesus is the only way to God.

Given the religious thought of today, this truth is unacceptable to many. They regard it as bigoted and a failure to recognize the worth of religions other than Christianity. The prevailing thought is that everyone is entitled to his opinion and that one religious opinion is as good as the next. A more unreasonable and absurd attitude it would be difficult to find. How can several diametrically opposed teachings on the way to God all be right? It is like a man in Edinburgh asking the way to London and being given the conflicting instructions to take a plane and fly west, take a boat and go east, take a train and go south. If he has any sense he will know that all the answers cannot be right. If he takes the trouble to look at a map he will be able to decide which piece of advice he should follow.

Accepting the truth that Jesus is the only way to God is not intolerant bigotry; it is simply believing the teaching God has given us in his Word. There Jesus said, 'I am the way and the truth and the life. No one comes to the Father except through me' (John 14:6).

The Apostle Peter said, 'Salvation is found in no one else, for there is no other name under heaven given to men by which we must be saved' (Acts 4:12).

The Apostle Paul said, 'For there is one God and one mediator between God and men, the man Christ Jesus' (1 Timothy 2:5).

Nothing is more clearly stated in the Bible. The quotes above can bear no interpretation other than that Jesus is the only way to God.

John 14:6 says very clearly and plainly states that there is only one way to come to God.

WHY?

It is God who is providing the way and what God does, he does perfectly right from the start. If we were doing it we would never get it right and would have to make improvements all the time.

It is for our peace of mind. If there were more than one way, we would never be sure that we had got the best way. We have the best way because there is only one way.

It is because of the nature of salvation. Salvation is from sin but man does not understand his sin. Therefore he cannot understand salvation. Man sees sin as a social blip, a temperamental hiccup, and not as a direct attack upon the person and integrity of God. He does not see it as a violation of God's law, nor as a contradiction to all that God stands for. Sin like this needs an infinite power to overcome it and only God can supply such a power.

The cost was so enormous that even God with his infinite resources could not have provided it twice. It took all that God had.

THE PROBLEM

The way to God and heaven is shut to us by our sin. That sin must be dealt with to God's satisfaction if a way is to be opened for sinners. Sin is a breaking of God's law and a rebellion against the authority of God. It is not merely a moral defect but an affront to the character and holiness of the Lord. Sin is a serious business and God's response to it is revealed in Genesis 6:5–6: 'The LORD saw how great man's wickedness on the earth had become, and that every inclination of the thoughts of his heart was only evil all the time. The LORD was grieved that he had made man on the earth, and his heart was filled with pain.'

God cannot be indifferent to sin and his opposition to it is not just that of a judge. His heart is the heart of a loving father pained and grieved by the waywardness of his children. For him to say that he was sorry he ever made man is a staggering acknowledgement. There is a very real sense in which when people sin, God suffers.

Human sin affects the relationship between God and man in two basic ways. Firstly, it brings upon us the wrath and condemnation of God. Secondly, it leaves us totally unable to meet God's requirements of love and obedience to his law and word. If a way is to be opened to God it must deal with both these problems. The way to God must be one that meets with God's full approval and satisfies the demands of God's law. Sin must be dealt with if we are ever to have a happy relationship with God. This problem is immense. It is completely beyond man to solve, even though history is full of his perverted ingenuity to obtain divine favour. If there is to be a solution, it is God who must provide it.

GOD'S REMEDY

In John 3:16, there is a perfect statement of God's remedy for sin: 'For God so loved the world that he gave his one and only Son, that whoever believes in him shall not perish but have eternal life.'

In his divine love, God provides a remedy which deals justly with the punishment that sin deserves and yet at the same time provides pardon for the sinner. God has said that the penalty for sin is death—spiritual and physical death. Nothing can change that because it is the judgement of the holy God. God will not turn a blind eye to our sin. Justice must be done, so the demands of God's law and the penalty for breaking that law must be satisfied.

In love and mercy God declares that he will accept a substitute to die in the sinner's place. But God's law demands that the substitute must be free from the guilt of sin and therefore not deserving of death himself. None of us could meet these requirements. So God sent his own Son into the world to become man and to keep his law fully and perfectly. This is what the man Jesus did, and thus became the only acceptable sacrifice to God for human sin.

This is why Jesus is the only way to God.

NO OTHER WAY

In John 14:6, the verse quoted above, Jesus is not saying that he is one of many ways to God but that he is the *only way*. There is a uniqueness and exclusiveness about Jesus when it comes to the matter of our salvation. There is a triple claim in that verse which is quite amazing. Jesus is *the* way and *the* truth and *the* life. There is no alternative to him and the second part of the verse confirms this: 'No one comes to the Father except through me.'

Why is Jesus so adamant that he is the only way to God? The stand he is taking requires that he be either totally deluded or totally correct. There is no room for half measure. Either Jesus is deluded and we can safely ignore him, or he is right and therefore it would be the greatest possible folly to ignore him. Our eternal destiny hangs upon this; so do we believe that Jesus is the only way to God?

WHAT ALTERNATIVE DO YOU HAVE?

Because of its hatred of one-way Christianity, the world has spent the past two thousand years looking for an alternative to Jesus. Self-effort, morality, all sorts of variations of Christianity and every conceivable alternative religion have been put forward. Well known people such as Prince Charles have supported this and in the event that he becomes king, he does not want to be known as Defender of *the* Faith, but Defender of faith.

All this has been useless in man's search for God so at last the final answer has supposedly been found—there is no God. Therefore we don't need a way to God.

But when man has made all his pronouncements about life and death and eternity, there still remains the great unalterable fact of GOD. And there is still only one way to know this God.

There is no alternative to Jesus.

That is where you are now. It is either Jesus or hell.

What a choice! In all the choices you have to make in life none is so clear and obvious as this. What is there to think about? It is obvious which to choose, but most people reject Jesus and are left with hell.

Why is this?

Here is evidence that the choice is not straightforward. There are forces at work to keep souls away from Jesus. But praise God there is a greater force to draw.

Ask God to overcome your natural desire to go the way of sin. Ask him to break down the pull of Satan. Ask him to conquer your will.

It is either Jesus or hell!

What a choice! But nothing is more clear than the Bible's way of salvation.

Appendix 3

ALL THINGS NEW—A help for those beginning the Christian life, 978-1850492269, Bryntirion Press

BEEP—Children's stories, 978-1894400107, Joshua Press

BELIEVERS NEED THE GOSPEL, 978-1879737426, Cavalry Press

BEN GROWS UP—Issues Ben faces as a teenager, 978-0852345283, Evangelical Press

BEN—Six illustrated children's stories, 978-1894400077, Joshua Press

BITESIZE THEOLOGY—An ABC of the Christian faith, 978-0852344477, Evangelical Press

CHAINS OF GRACE—Peter Jeffery's story, 978-1846251276, Day One Publications

CHRISTIAN HANDBOOK WORKBOOK—A study guide to be used with the Christian Handbook

CHRISTIAN HANDBOOK—A guide to the Bible, Church History and Christian Doctrine, 978-1850490654, Bryntirion Press

ENJOYING GOD ALWAYS—366 Daily Devotions, 978-0852345207, Evangelical Press

EVANGELICALS THEN AND NOW, 978-0852345641, Evangelical Press

FIRM FOUNDATIONS—Two months in the greatest Bible chapters, 978-1850490319 Bryntirion Press

FOLLOWING THE SHEPHERD IN PSALM 23, 978-1850491255, Bryntirion Press

FROM RELIGION TO CHRIST, 978-1879737136, Calvary Press

GREAT GOD OF WONDERS—The attributes of God for new believers, 978-0852343029, Evangelical Press

GROWING UP—Issues Ben faces as a teenager, 978-0852345283, Evangelical Press

HOW SHALL THEY HEAR—Church based evangelism, 978-0852343838, Evangelical Press

HOW TO BEHAVE IN CHURCH—Studies in 1 Timothy, 978-0852343180, Evangelical Press

I WILL NEVER BECOME A CHRISTIAN—Seven reasons challenged, 978-1846250262, Day One Publications

LIGHTS SHINING IN THE DARKNESS—Great men of church history, 978-0852345054, Evangelical Press

MOVING OUT WITH THE CHRISTIAN FAITH, 978-0852346099, Evangelical Press

NEW CHRISTIANS START HERE—The basic truths for the new believer, 978-0852345917, Evangelical Press

OPENING UP EPHESIANS, 978-0971016972, Evangelical Press/Solid Ground Christian Books

OPENING UP EZEKIEL'S VISIONS, 978-1903087664, Day One Publications

OUR PRESENT SUFFERING—Why do believers suffer?, 978-0900898761, Bryntirion Press

OVERCOMING LIFE'S DIFFICULTIES—Learning from the book of Joshua, 978-0852344347, Evangelical Press

PREACHERS WHO MADE A DIFFERENCE, 978-0852345757, Evangelical Press

RAINBOW OF GRACE—Learning from the life of Noah, 978-0852344194, Evangelical Press

SALVATION EXPOSED, 978-0852344675, Evangelical Press

SEEKING GOD—For those seriously seeking God, 978-1850491316, Bryntirion Press

SICKNESS AND DEATH IN THE CHRISTIAN FAMILY—John 11, 978-0852343081, Evangelical Press

STAND FIRM—The armour of God for young believers, 978-0900898877, Bryntirion Press

STEPPING STONES—A guide to the books of the New Testament for beginners, 978-0851515977, Banner of Truth

STRUGGLING BUT WINNING—How to cope with difficulties, 978-0852343371, Evangelical Press

THE BIGGEST ISSUE—Meeting God, past, present and future, 978-0852346716, Evangelical Press

THE CROSS, 978-0852346099, Evangelical Press

THE LORD'S SUPPER, 978-0852344026, Evangelical Press

THE TRUTH ABOUT CHRISTMAS, 978-0971016958, Evangelical Press

THE YOUNG SPURGEON—The story of the teenage Spurgeon, 978-0852342930, Evangelical Press

WALK WORTHY—For those beginning the Christian life, 978-1850491682, Bryntirion Press

Appendix 3

WHAT YOU NEED TO KNOW ABOUT SALVATION—A day-by-day guide to the Christian Faith, 978-0852343470, Evangelical Press

WHICH WAY TO GOD?, 978-0852344132, Evangelical Press

WHO WANTS TO BE A MILLIONAIRE?—And thirty-two other tracts, 978-1846250668, Day One Publications

WINDOWS OF TRUTH—Illustrations on the way of salvation and the Christian life, 978-0851516363, Banner of Truth

YOU CAN'T FOOL GOD, 978-0852344880, Evangelical Press

Open air preaching, Arizona, 1994

Peter and Lorna in Atlanta

Photo gallery

With the Dykstra family in New Jersey

With Mike Gaydosh

Playing golf in Australia

**Three pastors of
Ebenezer: Derek
Swann, Peter Jeffery
and Phil Williams**

Photo gallery

Israel, 1988

Peter and family on his 60th birthday

Opening up Ezekiel's visions

PETER JEFFERY

128PP, PAPERBACK

ISBN 978-1-90308-766-4

Ezekiel, a much neglected Old Testament prophet, speaks across the centuries in this straightforward and down-to-earth explanation of his message. Clearly written, with no punches pulled as far as contemporary application is concerned, this is just the sort of help needed by those who might otherwise find the book difficult to understand.

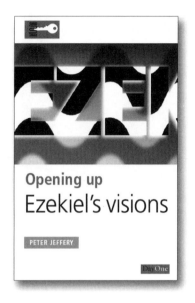

'Once again, Peter Jeffery has succeeded in bringing home to twenty-first century people God's ever relevant diagnosis of their condition and his remedy for it.'
GRAHAM HARRISON

I will never become a Christian

Seven reasons challenged

PETER JEFFERY

80PP, PAPERBACK

ISBN 978-1-84625-026-2

In a time when people offer excuses for responding to the gospel, Peter Jeffery provides plain answers in an easy-to-read style, considering objections such as All Christians are hypocrites, Christians can't even agree among themselves, A God of love could never allow suffering, and Being a Christian involves committing intellectual suicide.

Who wants to be a millionaire?

And 32 other tracts from Peter Jeffery

PETER JEFFERY

CD OF PRINTABLE TRACTS AND UPLOADABLE HTM FILES

ISBN 978-1-84625-066-8

In over thirty engagingly written and illustrated pieces, Peter Jeffery applies the good news of the Christian faith and teaching in a way you and others will love reading about it. These tracts are supplied on three formats: PDFs (US letter size for folding, and UK A4 size for folding) and as HTML text so you can load them on your website. Purchase of this CD licenses you or your church to print and distribute as many of these tracts as you wish, and to publish and circulate them electronically by e-mail or on the world wide web.

About Day One:

Day One's threefold commitment:

- To be faithful to the Bible, God's inerrant, infallible Word;
- To be relevant to our modern generation;
- To be excellent in our publication standards.

I continue to be thankful for the publications of Day One. They are biblical; they have sound theology; and they are relative to the issues at hand. The material is condensed and manageable while, at the same time, being complete—a challenging balance to find. We are happy in our ministry to make use of these excellent publications.
JOHN MACARTHUR, PASTOR-TEACHER, GRACE COMMUNITY CHURCH, CALIFORNIA

It is a great encouragement to see Day One making such excellent progress. Their publications are always biblical, accessible and attractively produced, with no compromise on quality. Long may their progress continue and increase!
JOHN BLANCHARD, AUTHOR, EVANGELIST AND APOLOGIST

Visit our website for more information and to request a free catalogue of our books.

www.dayone.co.uk